tarawa 1943

the turning of the tide

DERRICK WRIGHT

tarawa 1943

the turning of the tide

Praeger Illustrated Military History Series

PRAEGER

Westport, Connecticut
London

Library of Congress Cataloging-in-Publication Data

Wright, Derrick, 1928–
    Tarawa 1943: the turning of the tide / Derrick Wright.
        p. cm – (Praeger illustrated military history, ISSN 1547-206X)
    Originally published: Oxford: Osprey, 2000.
    Includes bibliographical references and index.
    ISBN 0-275-98271-8 (alk. paper)
    1. Tarawa, Battle of, Kiribati, 1943. I. Title. II. Series.
    D767.917.W77   2004
    940.54'26681–dc22 2003063215

British Library Cataloguing in Publication Data is available.

First published in paperback in 2000 by Osprey Publishing Limited, Elms Court,
Chapel Way, Botley, Oxford OX2 9LP. All rights reserved.

Library of Congress Catalog Card Number: 2003063215
ISBN: 0-275-98271-8
ISSN: 1547-206X

Praeger Publishers, 88 Post Road West, Westport, CT 06881
An imprint of Greenwood Publishing Group, Inc.
www.praeger.com

Printed in China through World Print Ltd.

The paper used in this book complies with the Permanent Paper Standard issued
by the National Information Standards Organization (Z39.48-1984).

10 9 8 7 6 5 4 3 2 1

ILLUSTRATED BY: Howard Gerrard

CONTENTS

ORIGINS OF THE CAMPAIGN

The arrival of Commodore Matthew Perry's flotilla of 'black ships' in Tokyo Bay in 1853 heralded Japan's emergence as a modern power after centuries of self-imposed feudalism. Once they had become convinced that protective isolation had to be abandoned if they were to evolve, the Japanese adopted a European style constitution during the reign of Emperor Meiji, and by 1890 a form of parliament, the Diet, had been established although the real power remained in the hands of shadowy military cliques and advisers interposed between the Emperor and his cabinet.

Expansion became a priority as the population burgeoned, and natural resources diminished. The Bonin Islands, the Kuriles, and Okinawa were annexed, and in 1894 the Korean government was overthrown and a puppet regime appointed. By 1904 disagreements with Russia over spheres of influence in Manchuria and Korea led to an undeclared war. Japan scored spectacular military successes at Port

Arthur, and at the great naval battle of Tsushima where the Russian fleet was destroyed for minor Japanese losses.

The outbreak of World War I afforded further opportunities for expansion without serious involvement. Siding with the Allies enabled Japan to absorb German holdings in China, and the islands of the central Pacific. The Treaty of Versailles in 1919 ceded Saipan and Tinian in the Marianas, as well as the Carolines and Marshall Islands, affording an outer ring of defensive locations that would prove invaluable after 1941.

The Washington Naval Conference of 1921–2 sought to prevent a naval dominance in the Pacific by any single power by limiting the tonnage of the American, British, and Japanese fleets. But by the late 1920s Japan had become disillusioned with the treaty, seeing the extra tonnage allowed to America and Britain, for their Atlantic commitments, as a humiliation.

China had long been viewed as a vast source of raw materials, and in 1931 the blowing up of a section of the Japanese-owned Manchurian railway was seized upon as an excuse for intervention, on the pretext of protecting Japanese lives and property. Relations with the West steadily deteriorated with the withdrawal from the League of Nations in 1933, and the renunciation of the Washington Naval Treaty in 1935. All-out war with China broke out in 1937, and Japan embarked on a huge naval expansion program laying down the keels of what were to be the world's two largest battleships, the *Yamato* and the *Musashi*, each of 72,000 tons.

Territorial gains in China were rapid and extensive, and when the war in Europe began in 1939, Japanese troops moved into the French colonies in Indo-China (Vietnam). Allied to Germany and Italy by the Tripartite Pact of 1940, Japan also secured her northern borders with a non-aggression pact with the Soviet Union in 1941. Viewing the situation with mounting unease, the United States froze Japanese assets in America, while Britain and the Dutch East Indies imposed a total ban on oil exports which denied her 90 per cent of her requirements. The seeds of war had been sown, and the appointment of the belligerent

Gen Hideki Tojo as Prime Minister in October 1941 accelerated the rush toward hostilities.

For decades the United States Navy had carried out its Pacific exercises in accordance with 'Plan Orange,' a thinly disguised code-name for war in Japan. It was recognized that Japan was the only country in the Pacific capable of mounting an attack on the United States and its bases, and the only one with any reason for doing so. How the attack on Pearl Harbor on December 7 1941 came as a surprise is in itself astonishing.

The brainchild of Adm Yamamoto, a veteran of the great battle of Tsushima and a champion of naval air power, the attack inflicted staggering damage to America's Pacific fleet and sent shock-waves throughout the country. The 'date that will live in infamy' heralded America's commitment to war against Japan, Germany, and Italy and marked the great turning point of World War II.

After Pearl Harbor, the first year of the Pacific War was a catalogue of disasters for the Allies. Land and air attacks against the Philippines resulted in the surrender of the islands in April 1942, and the undignified evacuation of Gen MacArthur; the British warships HMS *Prince of Wales* and HMS *Repulse* fell victim to Japanese aircraft and were sunk off northern Malaya in December; Guam and Wake Island fell in the same month. In February the British bastion of Singapore was surrendered by the hapless Gen Arthur Percival.

In January the Japanese invaded Burma and New Guinea, and by March the Dutch East Indies, with their massive oil reserves, had been occupied. It was not until May of 1942 that the tide of expansion was checked. A Japanese invasion fleet heading for Port Moresby in New

A Japanese 7.7 mm light machine gun, of similar design to the British Bren gun. They were found by the hundred on Betio Island. (National Archives)

Guinea was intercepted by Adm Fletcher's Task Force 17, and in the ensuing Battle of the Coral Sea, both sides lost an aircraft carrier; the Japanese *Shoho* and the American USS *Lexington*. Although not a decisive victory for the Americans the battle achieved the indefinite postponement of the landings at Port Moresby.

Under the pretext of mounting an invasion of the tiny atoll of Midway, Yamamoto hoped to lure the remains of the US Navy into a full-scale battle, in which the overwhelming superiority of the Imperial Navy would triumph. However he was unaware that American cryptanalists had succeeded in decoding nearly 90 per cent of Japanese message traffic dealing with the Midway operation. This allowed a smaller US fleet, under Adms Fletcher and Spruance, to secure a tactical advantage which resulted in the sinking of four Japanese aircraft carriers for the loss of one American. Now recognized as the turning point of the Pacific War, the Battle of Midway marked the juncture at which the Japanese tide of expansion was contained. From the summer of 1942, the enemy were first held, and then defeated, in savage fighting in New Guinea by American and Australian troops, while the marines of the 1st Division fought a harrowing battle at Guadalcanal in the Solomon Islands.

The Casablanca Conference in 1943 confirmed the Allies' determination to make the defeat of Germany their prime objective, but it was also decided to step up the offensive in the Pacific. At a Pacific Military Conference in Washington in March, Gen MacArthur urged a south to north advance, via New Guinea and the Philippines, while Adms King and Nimitz favored an 'island-hopping' strategy through the central Pacific. Both options were given tacit approval by the Joint Chiefs of Staff, and Nimitz, with the assistance of Adm Spruance, began preparations for an amphibious assault on the enemy's outer defensive perimeter sometime in November 1943.

Utilizing the islands and atolls ceded to them after World War I, Japan had constructed an outer ring of defenses, ranging from the Marinas, the Palaus and the Carolines, to the Marshall Islands in the east. Truk, in the central Carolines, became the principal naval base—the Gibraltar of the Pacific.

An attack on the island of Makin in the northern Gilbert Islands, by a Marine Raider Battalion in August 1942, alerted the Japanese to the vulnerability of the Gilberts, and the token force in the area was reinforced by a much larger contingent of troops. The island of Betio (pronounced 'baysho') on the atoll of Tarawa was selected as a main base as it afforded the best site for an airfield, and construction battalions began building the island's defenses in September.

Lying some 2,500 miles (4,020km) southwest of Hawaii and 1,300 miles (2,100km) south east of Truk, Tarawa had a unique location. To the north and west lay the Marshall and Caroline Islands, while south and east were the Allied-held bases. As the most southerly point in Japan's outer defense ring it held a pivotal position on the lifeline from Hawaii and the United States to the South Pacific, Australia and New Zealand. It was vital that this lifeline be maintained and most Allied operations in 1942 and early 1943 were conducted to that end. The invasion of Guadalcanal in 1942 and the operations in Papua New Guinea steadily rolled back the Japanese forward positions that threatened Australia.

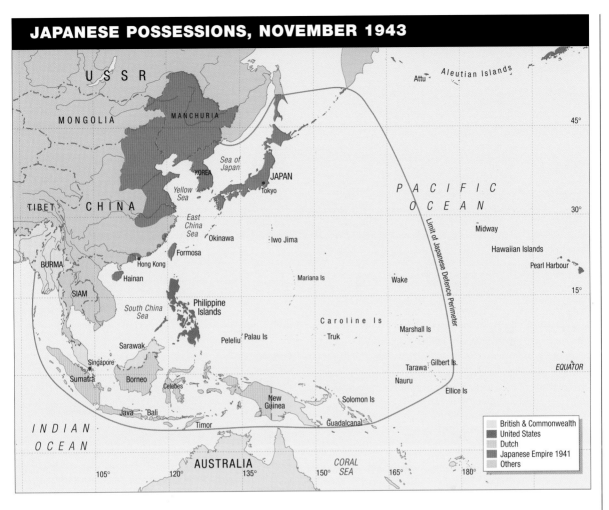

Initially the Marshall Islands were to have been the first objective in the central Pacific drive. Ceded to Japan after the First World War, little was known of their defenses, but they were believed to have been strong and the garrison large. The relatively close proximity of Truk posed a threat of land and naval intervention and Spruance and his planning team were reluctant to take the risk in what was to be the Marines' pioneering amphibious assault against the enemy. America was frantically rebuilding its navy after the Pearl Harbor attack, but it was still not strong and the landing force would rely heavily on obsolete ships for support. The decision was made to assault an island that could be readily taken with whatever resources were available at the time; a flawed decision as events were to subsequently prove.

The Gilberts had until recently been British territory and the Americans had access to a wide range of up-to-date information about the islands from British and Commonwealth expatriates. At a conference held in Hawaii in September 1943, Operation Galvanic: the invasion of Tarawa, Makin and the small island of Apamama, was formulated and the first of the 'island hopping' operations was approved.

At this stage of the war nobody knew if such a complex and perilous undertaking would succeed at all or at what cost. It would soon be the task of the Marine Corps 2nd Division to find out.

CHRONOLOGY

1941

December 7	Japanese aircraft attack Pearl Harbor. US declares war on Japan.
December 8	Japanese attack the Philippines, Hong Kong, Malaya, and Wake Island.
December 10	HMS *Prince of Wales* and HMS *Repulse* sunk off the east coast of Malaya.
December 11	Germany and Italy declare war on the United States.
December 24	Japanese troops occupy Wake Island.
December 25	Hong Kong surrenders to the Japanese.
December 31	Japanese troops advance on Manila, the Philippines capital.

1942

January 16	Japanese troops cross over Burmese border.
February 15	Gen Percival surrenders Singapore to Gen Yamashita.
March 12	Gen MacArthur is evacuated from the Philippines.
May 4–7	Battle of Midway, turning point of the Pacific War.
May 6	All US forces in the Philippines surrender.
May 7	Battle of the Coral Sea, Japanese troops prevented from landing at Port Moresby.
May 15	Last British troops withdraw across the Burma–India border.
August 7	US Marines land at Guadalcanal in the Solomon Islands.
August 17	US Marine Raider Battalion attacks Makin Island in the Gilberts.
October 11	Naval battle off Cape Esperance, Guadalcanal.

1943

January 4	Japanese evacuation of Guadalcanal gets under way.
February 1	All Japanese troops leave Guadalcanal.
March 2–5	Naval battle of Bismarck Sea, Japanese convoy sunk off Lae.
April 18	Adm Yamamoto shot down and killed over Bougainville by US fighters.
June 30	Operation Cartwheel, amphibious operations against Japanese in Solomon Is.
September	Conference in Hawaii, formulation of Operation Galvanic.
August 28	Japanese evacuate New Georgia in Solomon Is.
November 1	2nd Marine Division leaves Wellington, New Zealand, for Tarawa
November 13	Convoy leaves New Hebrides with 27th Infantry Division.
November 20	Battle of Tarawa, D-day.
0300hrs	Transports begin disembarking troops.
0441hrs	Red star shell indicates Japanese are on Betio.
0500hrs	Kingfisher spotter plane launched; Japanese fire on *Maryland*.
0530hrs	Troopships affected by southerly current.
0600hrs	Minesweepers begin clearing entrance to lagoon.
0735hrs	Main bombardment by support group.
0900hrs	Troops begin to land.
late afternoon	Salvo from *Ringgold* and *Dashiell* kills Adm Shibasaki and his staff.
November 21	D-day+1 6th Marines come ashore.
afternoon	Japanese troops spotted moving to Bairiki.
2030hrs	Col Merrit Edson comes ashore and takes over command.
November 22	D-day+2 Major Hays' 1-8 begin assault on the 'Pocket'.
November 23	D-day+3
0300hrs	'Banzia' charge to 1-6 defenses.
0700– 0730hrs	Destroyers bombard remaining garrison.
1300hrs	Eastern end of island in US control. The 'Pocket' falls. Collapse of Japanese opposition on Betio.
November 24	Stars and Stripes and Union Jack raised.
November 27	Remaining Japanese on Na'a defeated - the battle for Tarawa is finally over.

OPPOSING COMMANDERS

Fleet Admiral Chester W. Nimitz. One of World War II's great leaders and Commander-in-Chief Pacific (CINCPAC), Nimitz was to oversee the Marine Corps' 'island-hopping' campaign throughout the Pacific War. By 1945 he not only commanded six Marine divisions, but also the largest navy the world has ever seen. (US Navy)

AMERICAN

As a branch of the navy, the operations of the United States Marine Corps in the Pacific came under the direct control of Adm Chester W. Nimitz, Commander-in-Chief Pacific (CINCPAC). Nimitz was a quiet, studious man, and an outstanding leader. At the close of the Pacific War he was in command of 21 admirals and generals, 6 marine divisions, 5,000 aircraft, and the biggest navy the world had ever seen. Rushed to Hawaii after the Pearl Harbor disaster, he relieved his predecessor, Adm Husband Kimmel, who together with his army counterpart, MajGen Walter Short, had been censured for the debacle. It is now widely believed that the pair were scapegoats for errors of judgement made at a much higher level.

A Texan of German descent, born in Fredericksburg in 1885, he joined the submarine service in 1908, and remained in that branch until the end of World War I. After various inter-war postings, the outbreak of World War II found him in Washington as chief of the Bureau of Navigation from where he was appointed CINCPAC ahead of Kimmel's immediate replacement VAdm Pye. Nimitz was particularly admired for his gift for dealing with volatile colleagues, as was demonstrated in his wartime association with the conceited and arrogant Douglas MacArthur, who frequently railed about the impracticality of the Marines' 'island-hopping' strategy. He was unquestionably the most important Allied military leader in the Pacific, and America's greatest ever admiral. He succeeded Adm King as Chief of Naval Operations after the signing of the Japanese surrender, and from 1949 worked as a goodwill ambassador for the United Nations, until his retirement in 1952. He died in San Francisco in 1966, aged 81.

His immediate superior, Adm Ernest King, Chief of Naval Operations, was as different from Nimitz as could be imagined. Arrogant, conceited, and foul-tempered, he was heartily disliked by almost everyone who came into contact with him. Churchill loathed him, and Eisenhower was once heard to say that the best way to hasten the end of the war would be to get someone to shoot Ernie King.

A notorious anglophobe, his dismissal of British intelligence reports pinpointing the movements of the German U-boats off the East Coast of America, was the direct cause of the loss of many Allied and American merchant ships and their crews. Happily, his involvement in Operation Galvanic was minimal. He approved the operation in general, but initially asked for Nauru, an island of little strategic importance some 250 miles (400km) to the west of Tarawa, to be included. Spruance was horrified and said that it would need an extra division for the operation. King's request was finally omitted, much to the relief of the planners.

MajGen Holland M. Smith (left), overall commander of the V Marine Amphibious Corps (VMAC), and MajGen Julian Smith (right), commander of the 2nd Marine Division. Holland Smith's deceptively benign appearance hid an explosive temper that earned him the nickname 'Howlin' Mad Smith.' (USMC)

Shortly before the Battle of Midway in May 1942, the commander of Task Force 16, Adm 'Bull' Halsey, was forced into hospital with a severe case of dermatitis. When Nimitz asked him to name his replacement he opted for VAdm Raymond Spruance. The choice was a surprise to Nimitz, and a shock to many senior officers who had not anticipated the appointment. As a mere cruiser division commander, and well known as a reserved and introverted character, it appeared to be a rather bizarre option. But Spruance's outstanding qualities surfaced during the battle, and Nimitz was quick to appreciate them; for the rest of the war he would act as the CINCPAC's chief strategist and right-hand man, planning almost every amphibious landing up to Okinawa.

The Marines for the operation, the V Marine Amphibious Corps (VMAC), were under the overall command of MajGen Holland M. Smith. His benign, grandfatherly appearance belied an explosive temper that prompted his Marines to adopt his initials 'H. M.' to 'Howlin' Mad,' a title that stuck for his entire career.

Smith was a champion of amphibious warfare, and had helped pioneer the techniques years earlier in the Caribbean. The outbreak of war found him in charge of Army and Marine amphibious training on America's West Coast, and he immediately became the prime choice for 'Galvanic.'

The assault on Betio was allocated to the 2nd Marine Division under its commander, MajGen Julian C. Smith. He was an unassuming and

Models of Betio Island, codenamed 'Helen', are displayed before the landings. (National Archives)

Col David M. Shoup. As divisional operations officer he planned the assault on Betio Island and was unexpectedly given the job of implementing his own plans. Shoup was awarded the Medal of Honor for his role in the battle, and in 1959 was appointed Commandant of the US Marine Corps. (USMC)

experienced officer, with 34 years' service behind him including a spell fighting the 'banana wars' – clandestine battles fought in the jungles of Haiti and Nicaragua in the 1920s and 1930s against revolutionaries. It was there that Smith won the Navy Cross. Although he played a role in the Peleliu battle in 1944, Tarawa was to be the pinnacle of his military career. He retired as a lieutenant general in 1946, and died in 1975 aged 90.

Getting the Marines to the Gilberts, and putting them ashore was the job of the Commander of Task Force 54, RAdm Richmond Kelly Turner. Short-tempered and foul-mouthed, he was generally referred to as 'Terrible Turner.' Born in Oregon in 1885 he was a master of the art of amphibious warfare, and organized the landings on Guadalcanal in 1942. Blessed with a phenomenal memory, which allowed him to absorb sheaves of paperwork at a single reading, his expertise was in demand throughout the Pacific campaign as a Commander of Amphibious Forces, Pacific Fleet. By 1945 he had overseen the landings in the Gilberts, New Georgia, the Marianas, Iwo Jima, and Okinawa.

At a lower command level there were several officers whose contribution has been recognized as very significant to the success of 'Galvanic.'

Col David M. Shoup was 38 at the time of the battle, and had only limited combat experience. He was the divisional operations officer responsible for planning the attack down to the last detail. He had devised a unique method of determining the number of Japanese on the island by equating the number of latrines shown on the aerial photographs to the number of backsides they could accommodate – his figures later proved to be amazingly accurate.

The final rehearsals for the landings on Tarawa were carried out at Efate in the New Hebrides. The designated leader of Regimental Landing Team 2, Col William Marshall, suffered a heart attack, and Shoup was given the job of implementing his own plans. Although wounded coming ashore, after Shoup landed on D-day he immediately set up a command post and directed operations throughout the most critical period of the battle, until relieved on November 21 by Edson. His leadership and devotion to duty won him the Medal of Honor, and he went on to a distinguished career, being appointed Commandant of the Marine Corps by President Eisenhower in 1959.

Another key role was played by Maj Michael Ryan, CO of L Company of the 2nd Marines. When his Battalion Commander, Maj Schoettel, failed to land on Red Beach 1 Ryan gathered together a mixture of scattered infantrymen, tank crews, amtrac drivers, engineers, and corpsmen and secured Green Beach at the western end of the island. The capture of this beach proved to be the single factor that turned the battle irrevocably in the favor of the Americans, earning Ryan a much deserved Navy Cross.

JAPANESE

Although the American command is well documented, that of the Japanese is less well known.

The Gilbert Islands came jointly under the control of the Commander-in-Chief, South East Asia, VAdm Kusaka, and the

This picture, showing rows of tetrahedrons off Green Beach in the foreground, and other barriers off the south coast, testifies to the large numbers of obstructions that were in place. (US Navy)

Commander-in-Chief 2nd Fleet, VAdm Kondo. Their sole contribution was to make the decision to reinforce the Gilberts, and to bolster the air detachments in the Solomons. Once Operation Galvanic was under way Tarawa was virtually abandoned.

As commander of the 111th Construction Unit, the placement of the defenses of Betio and the construction of the airfield fell to Lt Murakami. More an engineer than a fighting man, he performed a brilliant job and turned the island into what was, yard for yard, probably the best defended outpost in the Pacific.

Murakami's aim was to prevent the enemy from reaching the beaches. He knew that if the Americans could establish a landing force in substantial numbers at any point on the island it would only be a matter of time before the defenders would be overwhelmed. His obstacles included pyramid-shaped reinforced concrete tetrahedrons which were placed around half of the island on the coral reef, anti-boat barriers made of palm tree logs, and double-apron barbed wire.

Ashore were anti-tank ditches, dug a short distance back from the perimeter barricades, and extensive minefields: the Model 93 against personnel and the Model 99 (magnetic) against tanks and armored vehicles. Although Lt Murakami had insufficient time to complete all of the fortifications that he had planned (3,000 mines remained in storage on D-day), he turned Betio into what his compatriots called 'a hornet's nest for the Yankees.'

In September 1943, R/Adm Keiji Shibasaki took over command of the island and its defenders. Young and ambitious, he boasted that 'The Americans could not take Tarawa with a million men in a hundred years.' Himself a veteran of amphibious landings along the coast of China, he fully appreciated the difficulties facing the invader and planned accordingly. He made his top priority the defense of the southern and western coastlines, confident that this was where the Americans would land. When they attacked from the lagoon side of Betio he took advantage of the lull in the naval bombardment, as the first waves of amtracs were approaching the beaches, to move as many of his weapons as he could to the northern shore.

Although Adm Shibasaki could only count around 3,000 of his garrison as effective combat troops, the remainder were very efficiently used to contribute to the defence of the island. The official history of the campaign states: 'Tarawa was the most heavily defended atoll that would ever be invaded by Allied forces in the Pacific and, with the possible exception of Iwo Jima, Betio was better protected against a landing force than any encountered in any theatre of war throughout WWII.'

Shibasaki's major contribution came before the Marines ever set foot on Betio, in training and motivating his defenders superbly. In retrospect it was a huge bonus to the Marines that he died so early in the battle as all evidence suggests that he would most certainly have ordered a major counter-attack on the first night, when the Marines were at their most vulnerable.

Rear Admiral Keiji Shibasaki. Young, experienced, and ruthless, Shibasaki's death on D-day was a fatal blow to the Japanese command on Betio, and doubtlessly altered the course of the battle. Had he survived to mount a counter-attack on the Marine positions that night the battle could have ended disastrously for the Americans. (War History Office, Defence Agency, Japan)

OPPOSING ARMIES

Despite a long history stretching back to the War of Independence, the United States Marine Corps had only limited experience of amphibious warfare by the end of 1943. In the inter-war years the techniques and logistics had been examined by leading Marines but the only practical experience to date had been at New Britain, New Guinea, and Guadalcanal where the landings had been opposed only lightly, if at all.

At Tarawa the plan was for the Marines to assault an island that was known to be heavily defended. The outcome would decide the whole future of the navy's proposed 'island-hopping' strategy for the remainder of the Pacific War. Although Holland Smith would subsequently dispute the value of Tarawa as a naval or military facility, it was accepted that the Gilberts were an essential stepping-off point for operations in the Marshall Islands. More importantly, the experience gained in the operation would be essential for the future.

The Japanese, on the other hand, were the acknowledged leaders in the field, having carried out many seaborne attacks, beginning in 1937 along the coast of China and, after the attack on Pearl Harbor, along the Malayan coast and in the Philippines. Adm Shibasaki had directed many such operations.

The 2nd Division, United States Marine Corps

After fighting alongside the 1st Division at Guadalcanal, the 2nd Division was transported to Wellington, New Zealand, for rest and rehabilitation in March 1943. Depleted more by illness than by enemy action (there were 1,300 confirmed cases of malaria), the division awaited replacements from America, and instituted a progressive training program which emphasized small unit tactics and amphibious assaults. At the time of Operation Galvanic the 2nd Division numbered around 20,000 men, composed of three infantry regiments, the 2nd, 6th and 8th (the USMC traditionally refer to their regiments simply as 'Marines').

An average regiment would comprise about 3,500 officers and men, and would have three rifle battalions consisting of three rifle companies, one weapons company, and one HQ company. The rifle and weapons companies were identified alphabetically, and each had three rifle platoons and one weapons platoon. The rifle platoon usually had 40 men divided into three 12-man squads with a platoon HQ.

The battalion weapons company had three .30 inch (7.6mm) machine gun platoons with six guns each, and a 3.2 inch (81mm) mortar platoon with six mortars. The battalion HQ company incorporated staff officers, clerks, and specialized units such as a navy medical section as well as air, artillery, and naval observers.

The division's fourth regiment, the 10th Marines, was the artillery who at the time had three 12-gun (3 inch; 75mm) pack howitzer

battalions, a 4 inch (105mm) medium howitzer battalion, and a 6 inch (155mm) heavy gun battalion, the whole being commanded by the regimental HQ.

The fifth regiment was the 18th Marines, made up of a battalion each of combat engineers, pioneers, and Seabees (construction battalions). The engineers were trained to construct or destroy fortifications, roads, and bridges, while the pioneers, although trained as combat troops, were primarily concerned with loading and unloading supplies. There were additional organic units within the division. A tank battalion of three companies of three tank platoons was using the Sherman M4-A2 medium tank. These were ideal for use against the Japanese in the Pacific where they completely outclassed the Japanese 'Ha-Go' tanks, but were not so successful in the European theater against German armor. There was also a medical battalion (largely staffed by navy doctors and corpsmen), and the amphibian tractor battalion who were the first to use the improved LVT-2 tractor the Tarawa operation. Universally known as the amtrac, it was originally designed by Donal Roebling as a rescue craft for the Florida Everglades. The amphibian tractor was ordered by the navy's Bureau of Shipping in 1941 to transport supplies from ship to shore, but it was soon adopted as an assault craft and was employed in a variety of roles throughout the Pacific.

The Marines at Tarawa, unlike those who fought at Guadalcanal, had modern infantry weapons including Garand M-1 semi-automatic rifles,

Japanese Type 95 'Ha-Go' tanks were inferior to the American Shermans in all respects. Many were used as static artillery pieces. This one, in a log revetment, is being examined by Marines after the battle. (US Navy)

Browning automatic rifles, and portable flame-throwers. A typical combat load would include; knapsack, poncho, entrenching tool, bayonet, K-bar knife, field rations, medical kit, and a gas mask (which was usually discarded). Others would carry heavier loads including ammunition, heavy weapons, and radios.

As replacements flowed in from America, the scale of training operations was accelerated with frequent amphibious exercises at Hawke Bay.

The United States Navy

From the time of their embarkation in Wellington on November 1, until they left the line of departure for the invasion beaches, the Marines of Holland Smith's V Amphibious Corps (VMAC) were the responsibility of the US Navy. The invasion force – Task Force 54 – was subdivided into two groups: the Northern Attack Force (Task Force 52) under VAdm Richmond Kelly Turner, which was to secure the island of Makin to the north; and the Southern Attack Force (Task Force 53) under RAdm Harry Hill, which would take Tarawa Atoll.

'Handsome' Harry Hill's force was made up of Transport Group 4 which included 13 attack transports (APAs) – the *Zeilen, Haywood, Middleton, Biddle, Lee, Monrovia, Sheridan, LaSalle, Doyen, Harris, Bell, Ormsby,* and *Feland* – and the attack cargo ships (AKAs) *Thuben, Virgo,* and *Bellatrix.*

The fire support group, under RAdm H. F. Kingman, comprised the battleships (BBs) *Tennessee, Maryland,* and *Colorado;* the heavy cruisers (CAs) *Portland* and *Indianapolis;* the light cruisers (CLs) *Mobile, Birmingham,* and *Santa Fe;* and the destroyers (DDs) *Bailey, Frazer, Gansevoort, Meade, Anderson, Russell, Ringgold, Dashiell,* and *Schroeder.* The three battleships of the group were semiobsolete ships that had been salvaged from the mud of Pearl Harbor after the 1941 attack. The *Maryland,* which would operate as the command ship and communications center, dated from the turn of the century, and like the others was too slow to accompany the fast Task Forces that now roamed the Pacific. However, they still packed a hefty punch with their 14 inch (356mm) and 16 inch (406mm) guns, and were ideally suited to provide offshore bombardments.

For air cover, aerial bombing, and strafing during the operation, three aircraft carriers (CVs), the *Essex, Bunker Hill,* and *Independence,* of RAdm A. E. Montgomery's Task Force 50-3 would accompany the Southern Attack Force. From Wellington, the invasion force sailed to Efate, in the New Hebrides, where the final amphibious rehearsals were carried out at Mele Bay. After refueling, the armada weighed anchor on November 13, and on the 17th rendezvoused with the convoy sailing from Hawaii with the army's 27th Infantry Division, bound for Makin.

Japan's Special Naval Landing Forces

The Tarawa battle would see the first confrontation between the US Marines and Japan's Special Navy Landing Force (SNLF)—sometimes referred to as the 'Imperial Marines.' The SNLF could trace its origins to the earliest days of the Imperial Japanese Navy when they were developed as small infantry units attached to naval ships. Over the years, however, they evolved into much larger combat units of highly trained and specialized amphibious infantry. In 1941 they spearheaded the invasions of Guam, Wake Island, and the Solomons. By 1942 there were over 50,000 *rikusentai* spread throughout the islands and atolls of the Pacific.

On Betio Island, RAdm Shibasaki commanded the 3rd Special Base Defence Force (formerly the 6th Yokosuka SNLF), the Sasebo 7th SNLF, the 111th Construction Unit, and a detachment of the 4th Fleet Construction Department; in all around 5,000 men. Because of the small area of the island, a considerable amount of which was taken up by the airfield and its facilities, Shibasaki concentrated his efforts on defeating the invader at the water's edge. Consequently the beach defenses were formidable.

Pride of place went to four 8 inch (203mm) naval guns situated at Temakin Point, and near Takarongo Point. For decades these guns were referred to as the 'Singapore' guns, as it was assumed that they were British Vickers guns that had been captured at Singapore and shipped to Betio Island. However, in 1974 a United Nations Advisor, William Bartsch, visited Betio and examined the guns, taking details of the hard stamped identification numbers. These were later identified by Vickers as part of an order supplied to Japan in 1905 at the time of the Russo-Japanese war.

Mistakenly referred to as the 'Singapore' guns, these British Vickers 8 inch (203mm) guns were sited at Temakin Point and near Takarongo Point. Silenced early in the battle by US Navy gunfire they played a minor role.

All along the island's coastline were a series of strongpoints, pill-boxes, and gun emplacements with integrated fields of fire. Most were encased in concrete and coral sand which proved to be effective protection, defying direct hits by bombs and shells. Scores of trenches, machine gun nests, and rifle pits were sited to provide interlocking fields of fire to sweep the beaches and the water beyond. Offshore, a double line of barbed-wire stretched out to the reef, and concrete tetrahedrons studded the water line.

Mobile armor was provided by seven Type 95 tanks, each mounting a 1.4 inch (37mm) cannon and two .3 inch (7.7mm) machine guns. Concrete bunkers, heaped over with sand and resembling small hillocks, were scattered around the island housing communication centers and ammunition dumps. Anti-tank ditches were placed around the airfield, and at the southeast and southwest tips of the island.

The orders for the Japanese garrison were unambiguous: 'If the enemy starts a landing, knock out the landing boats with gunfire, tank guns, and infantry guns, then concentrate all fire on the enemy's landing point and destroy him at the water's edge.'

OPPOSING PLANS

AMERICAN

A major factor of the Tarawa battle was speed: Nimitz ordered Spruance to 'get the hell in there, and get the hell out,' and Spruance urged 'lightning speed' upon the 2nd Division commander.

The fear of a major Japanese naval retaliation was paramount in the thinking behind this, the first of the Marines' 'island-hopping' campaigns. Kelly Turner and Holland Smith both accompanied the Northern Attack Force in their assault on Makin Island, although it was clear that Tarawa was going to be the major battle. If the Japanese intended to attack V Amphibious Corps the threat would be from the north, and the navy wanted its most experienced commanders to be available to deal with any contingency.

However, a series of US offensives in the Solomon Islands in early 1943 had caused the Japanese to divert ships and aircraft from as far away as the Marshalls, the Marianas, and the Celebes, to counter a very real threat against their stronghold of Rabaul. The Imperial Navy took a serious view of the threat, and transferred a large number of ships from Truk to bolster the Rabaul defenses. As a result the 22nd Air Flotilla, and the naval forces in the Marshalls, were so weakened that they were incapable of repelling any major landings in the area.

The Gilbert Islands had been under British jurisdiction since 1915, and consequently the Marine planners were able to draw upon the experience of a number of British, Australian, and New Zealand expatriates whom they named the 'foreign legion.' The maps and charts of the islands dated from the turn of the century and were very unreliable. The submarine USS *Nautilus* had surveyed the area, taking photographs and noting defenses, but the all important subject of tides worried Shoup and his staff.

Betio Island was surrounded by a reef which extended for some 800–1,200 yards (758–1,092m) out to sea. The first three waves of 1,500 men were due to land in amtracs (LVTs), therefore the depth of water around the island was, theoretically, irrelevant. However, the remainder would come ashore in Higgins boats – Landing Craft Vehicle Personnel (LCVPs) – shallow-draught, 36-foot (11m) long boats with wide ramps, they drew only 3–4 feet (910–1,200mm) of water when loaded.

Opinions among the 'foreign legion' were varied; some thought that there would be enough water to allow the Higgins boats to clear the reef, but there was one consistently dissenting voice. Maj Frank Holland had lived in the Gilberts for 15 years, and had made a hobby of studying the tides around the islands. When he heard that the Marines intended to land on Betio on November 20 he was appalled: he knew that there

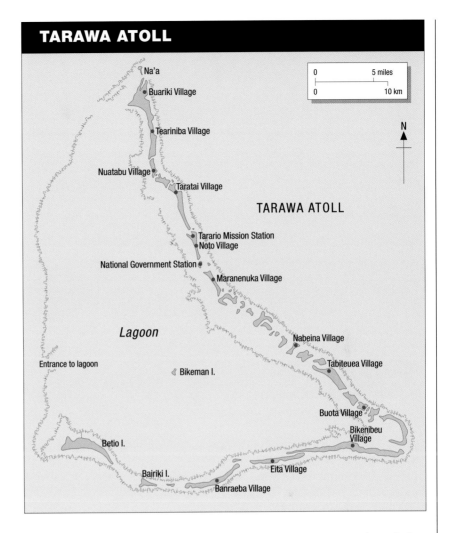

0 5 miles
0 10 km

Na'a
Buariki Village
Teariniba Village
Nuatabu Village
Taratai Village

N

TARAWA ATOLL

Tarario Mission Station
Noto Village
National Government Station
Maranenuka Village

Lagoon

Nabeina Village

Entrance to lagoon

Bikeman I.

Tabiteuea Village

Buota Village

Bikenibeu Village

Betio I.

Bairiki I.

Eita Village

Banraeba Village

would be a 'dodging' tide at that time, giving no more than 3 feet (910mm) of water over the reefs. If his predictions were correct the second wave of Higgins boats would ground, and the Marines would either have to be transferred to amtracs returning from the initial landing, or wade the rest of the way to the beaches on foot.

Julian Smith had intended to land with two regiments abreast and with one in reserve, but Holland Smith announced that the 6th Marines would be held as Corps reserves. This, coupled with a decision by Nimitz to limit the pre-invasion bombardment of Betio to around three hours on the morning of D-day (to achieve 'strategic surprise') meant that the Marines would be mounting a frontal attack with only a 2-1 superiority; well below the desired minimum.

Col Shoup and the 2nd Division planners had decided to attack from the lagoon side, which was minimally less well defended, and offered calmer waters for the amphibious assault craft. The assault plan was relatively straightforward. The transports would assemble to the west of the atoll and disembark the Marines. The landing craft would make their way to the boat rendezvous area, just outside of the gap in the western reef, from where they would move in predetermined waves to the line of departure some 7,000 yards (6,370m) inside the lagoon. From there the

Marines were released from navy control and the assault waves, headed by the amtracs, would make the final dash of around 6,000 yards (5,460m) to the beaches.

The three landing beaches were designated from west to east as Red 1, 2, and 3. The 3rd Battalion 2nd Marines (3-2), under Maj John Schoettel, were to land on Red 1: a deep cove, its eastern half was protected by a log barricade and covered from both sides by heavy machine guns and artillery. Red 2 stretched for about 500 yards (455m) from the eastern end of the cove to a quarter-mile (400m) long pier, and was assigned to the 2nd Battalion 2nd Marines (2-2), under LtCol Herbert Amey. There was a 3–4 foot high (910–1,200mm) log wall along the entire length of this beach, and from the pier to a point level with the end of the airfield runway. Red 3 stretched for 800 yards (728m) intersected by the short Burns-Philp pier; here the 2nd Battalion 8th Marines (2-8), under Maj Henry Crowe, would land.

The western end of Betio had been designated as Green Beach and the southern shore as Black 1 and 2 but no landings were planned here on D-day (see map on page 30).

Betio Island from the west. This picture gives a clear view of the reefs that surrounded the island and stretched for some 800–1,200 yards (728–1,092m) offshore. On the left is the cove of Red Beach 1, and the long wooden pier that intersected Red Beaches 2 and 3. (National Archives)

JAPANESE

Astute commander that he was, Adm Shibasaki probably realized that once the American force arrived, he and his garrison on Tarawa, the most southerly of Japan's outer defence ring, would be abandoned.

In the early stages of the war, the Americans had difficulty in

understanding the mentality of a people who were prepared to fight to

the death to defend untenable positions. But as the war ground on they learned that, for the vast majority of Japan's forces, surrender was not an option, and that they would have to be blasted and burned out of every single defensive position – prisoners were rare in the Pacific War.

Shibasaki's prime objective was to prevent the invader reaching the beaches. He knew his first defense was a natural one: the shelflike reef surrounding the whole island, which was to prove almost catastrophic to the Marines. At the water's edge a log barricade surrounded most of the island, and behind it, at strategic points, were coastal guns ranging in caliber from 3.1 inch (80mm) to 8 inch (203mm), dual-purpose anti-aircraft guns from 2.73 to 5 inch (70 to 127mm) and more than 30 other pieces ranging from 3 inch (75mm) pack howitzers to 1.4 inch (37mm) quick-firing, light field guns, 0.5 inch (13mm) machine guns, and a large number of 0.3 inch (7.7mm) infantry light machine guns (See map on page 46).

In the center of the island the airfield, with its 4,000 foot (1,213m) long runway, was dominant. The Admiral's command post, an impressive reinforced concrete structure measuring 25 x 60 x 40 feet (7.6 x 8.2 x 12.13m) stood some 500 yards (455m) inland from the Burns-Philp pier.

Anti-tank ditches were dug at both ends of the airfield and near to the 8 inch (203m) Vickers guns. Offshore concrete tetrahedrons and log and barbed-wire barricades were so placed that, by avoiding them, the landing craft would enter 'killing channels' covered by the main gun batteries.

Tarawa Atoll is roughly triangular in shape: a chain of over 25 small islands form the eastern side, and seven larger ones make up the southern base, with Betio at the western extremity. The western side of the triangle is mostly submerged reef with a half-mile (805m) wide navigable passage leading into a lagoon. Shibasaki and his engineers had concentrated the defenses on the southern shore of the island from where they expected the Marines to land.

THE BATTLE

D-DAY

In the pre-dawn darkness of November 20 the invasion fleet lay off the coast of Betio. It was so quiet that some optimists believed that the Japanese had abandoned the island: 'Try as I might I never got over the feeling that the Japs had pulled out of Tarawa – not until the first bullet whizzed by my ear,' said the noted war correspondent Robert Sherrod.

The planners had called for a raid on the island by B24 Liberator bombers of the 7th Air Force based at Funafuti in the Ellice Islands, to saturate the island with 500lb (225kg) bombs, fuzed to detonate a few fee above ground level. But the raid never materialized; this was the first of a number of 'foul-ups' that were to rob the Marines of an opportunity to cut back on the enemy's firepower on the beaches.

By 0300hrs the transports were in position and the long and laborious task of disembarking the troops and filling the landing craft got under way. The amtracs and LCVPs went into the water, came alongside the troop transports, and the precarious business of loading the Marines got under way. Although they had practiced many times before leaving New Zealand, the maneuver was fraught with danger. Climbing down netting on the side of a tall troopship, laden with anything up to 100 lb of equipment, in almost total darkness in a choppy sea was not the ideal way of leaving ship. With a wary eye on the man above, who may trample on your hands, and looking downward at the gap below as the landing craft slammed against the ship's hull, the Marines were very aware of the likelihood of falls or crushed limbs.

Breakfast for the Marines would be steak and eggs, a tradition that started in Australia with the 1st Division, and one that was frowned on by the navy doctors who knew that they would probably be treating many stomach wounds before the day was over.

Many eyes on the assembled ships were watching Betio, and at 0441hrs all heads turned as a single red-star shell shot into the sky from the center of the island; any lingering doubts about the Japanese presence were gone.

At around 0500hrs a Kingfisher spotter-plane was launched from Harry Hill's flagship the *Maryland*. Its job was to observe the imminent naval bombardment and radio back corrections to range and direction. Seeing the flash from the ship's catapult, the Japanese manning the 8 inch (203mm) gun at Temakin Point opened fire on the *Maryland*, overshooting by some 500 yards (455m). The battleships and cruisers swung around, and one battleship fired a salvo from its 16 inch (406mm) gun in retaliation. Marines in their landing craft watched in awe as the massive shells howled over their heads and crashed down just short of the beach.

RIGHT **One of the Vickers guns on Betio, this one at Takarongo Point. (Jim Moran)**

BELOW, RIGHT **Another of the 8 inch guns. (Jim Moran)**

The bombardment continued, the sky lit up with monstrous flashes, and an eerie silence was shattered as salvo after salvo thundered across the water: 'We do not intend to neutralize the island, we do not intend to destroy it, we will obliterate it,' said one admiral. The folly of his words would only be realized at the post-mortem after the battle.

Aboard the old battleship *Maryland*, the terrific concussion from the broadsides from the 16 inch (406mm) guns caused lights to go out and radios to malfunction. From that moment, until the end of the battle, communications between Harry Hill and the rest of his command would be a serious problem.

At 0530hrs it became evident that the troopships were out of position – a strong southerly current had carried them within range of the enemy shore batteries. The shelling was abruptly terminated as the ships scurried to their new positions, followed by flotillas of landing craft looking, as one observer put it, 'like ducklings following their mother.'

Admiral Shibasaki was now fully aware that the Americans intended to attack from the north. He was also aware of the problems still facing the enemy: the natural protection of the coral reef and the low tide that

Between October 1943 and January 1944, World War I veteran Kerr Eby (1890-1946) traveled with Marines in the South Pacific as part of Abbott Laboratories combat artist program, witnessing some of the fiercest fighting of the war, including landing with the invasion force at Tarawa. His drawings have become synonymous with the bloody fighting the Marines endured. Here the artist depicts a Higgins boat which has just grounded on the reef hundreds of yards offshore. The Marines are left with no alternative but to wade in through waist-high water against concentrated fire from positions that the Japanese had spent months preparing.

morning. When to his relief the massive bombardment suddenly stopped, he immediately began moving men and equipment from the southern shore to the north as his lookouts warned him of columns of landing craft heading for the channel in the reef that led to the lagoon.

Carrier aircraft were due to make a strike on Betio at 0550hrs but they were late. Hill was having difficulty in contacting the carriers which were some 10 miles (16km) offshore, and just as he was about to renew his attack without them, they arrived from the west. For seven minutes the Hellcat fighters and Avengers and Dauntless bombers ranged the length of the island, before wheeling away to rejoin the *Essex*, *Independence* and *Bunker Hill*.

Shortly after 0600hrs, the minesweepers *Pursuit* and *Requisite* began sweeping the entrance to the lagoon, and immediately came under fire from shore batteries. Once the passage was clear the destroyers *Ringgold* and *Dashiell* entered the lagoon and engaged the enemy with their 6 inch (152mm) guns. The *Ringgold* was struck twice by 5 inch (127mm) shells which luckily failed to explode. The *Pursuit* meanwhile took up position at the line of departure and shone her searchlight to guide the landing craft through the smoke drifting northward from Betio.

It was 0735hrs that the main bombardment by the support group got under way. In a spectacular display of pyrotechnics the battleships and cruisers raked the island from end to end; great gouts of sand and coral erupted, an ammunition dump exploded, and a huge column of black smoke from a fuel store rose into the morning sky.

Many Marines could have been forgiven for thinking that the Betio defenses had indeed been 'obliterated,' but the post-action review was to show that the navy had achieved few of its aims. The ground had been well and truly churned over, and some of the defenses were destroyed, but the bulk of the Japanese defenders and their weapons were still in place, awaiting the first wave of Marines. The navy were to eventually learn that their heavy ships were too close to the shore, and the resultant low trajectory caused many shells to simply bounce off the island and land in the sea.

It was now broad daylight, and the temperature was soaring; Tarawa is only 80 miles (125km) north of the equator, and November was the height of summer. Throughout the battle the Marines were to suffer from furnace-like heat and acute water shortages. In another of the numerous planning blunders that plagued the operation, it had been decided to utilize the oil drums to transport the drinking water, but inadequate cleaning somewhere along the line resulted in tainted water which caused countless cases of vomiting and stomach pains.

For the landing craft the haul to the beaches seemed unending. First they had to assemble between the transports and the entrance to the lagoon; from there it was a 3.5 mile (5.6km) trip to the line of departure and a further 3 miles (4.8km) to the beaches. By the time they landed some of the troops would have been pitching about on the sea for nearly six hours.

From his Kingfisher spotter plane, LtCdr MacPherson had had a spectacular view of the bombardment. He was now concerned by the slow progress of the landing craft; the delays in moving the transports, and a heavy swell, had slowed down the whole operation and Harry Hill was left with no option but to put back H-hour – the time the Marines were due on the beaches – to 0900hrs.

Adm Spruance in his flagship *Indianapolis* was off the south coast of the island. He had seen the air strikes and the bombardment, but had not been able to get in contact with Hill. To the best of his knowledge things were on schedule; he knew nothing of the delays caused by the movement of the transports and the postponement of H-hour.

At 0900hrs Harry Hill ordered the end of the bombardment. He was worried that the smoke and dust rising from the island would affect the accuracy of his gunfire, and that the LVTs now approaching the beaches would be hit. Julian Smith and his chief of staff, Merrit Edson, protested vigorously but to no avail. The result was that the Japanese had a vital ten minutes respite in which to reorganize and bring their guns to bear on the rows of lumbering craft now approaching the end of the pier.

In the first three waves were the amtracs: 42 LVT-1s, each carrying 18 men, and 45 LVT–2s, each holding 20 men. Behind them were three waves of Higgins boats straining to keep contact in the choppy seas.

For the Japanese, the approaching landing craft came as a big shock. Instead of the wooden boats that they were expecting they were confronted by rows of metal tractors, something akin to floating tanks, loaded with assault troops. To their amazement they did not ground on the reef but climbed over the coral and continued to the shore with all guns blazing.

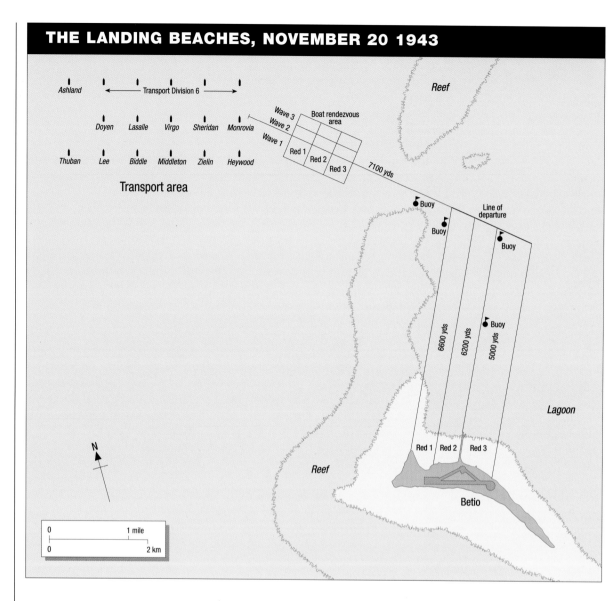

Braving anti-aircraft fire, LtCdr MacPherson dived in low ahead of the flotilla and took a look at the reef. What he saw filled him with horror: instead of the 4–5 feet (1.2–1.52m) of water they had been told to expect, the sea was so low that in places large areas of coral were drying in the sun while elsewhere it looked as if 3 feet (910mm) would be the most that could be expected. Maj Holland's predictions, largely ignored by the planners, would haunt many people before the end of D-day.

As the rows of amtracs labored toward the beaches, a lone boat was surging ahead; Lt William Hawkins and a group of his specially trained scout sniper platoon were heading for the end of the long wooden pier. Their task was to clear it of any Japanese who could fire on the landing craft which would shortly be passing on either side.

Hawkins' men were all experts in their field and their leader was ideally suited to the task. The 30-year-old Texan had won a field commission on Guadalcanal and was the first man to land on Betio.

Accompanied by engineering officer 2nd Lt Leslie and four other men, he climbed to the top of the wooden pier. Among a pile of fuel drums that were stacked near the end, the Japanese immediately opened fire with small arms but the group pressed forward, killing the defenders and destroying a number of wooden shacks with a flame-thrower carried by Leslie.

Unfortunately, the fire spread to the pier itself, eating its way through the planking and causing a gap that would slow down supply operations later in the battle. Other enemy positions were silenced including a machine-gun nest that had been built among the pier's timber supports.

With their mission complete, the scout snipers boarded their LCVP and attempted to get to the beach via a boat channel along the west side of the pier. However, the water proved to be too shallow and they were eventually forced to transfer to amtracs.

RED BEACH 1 – MORNING

As the amtracs of the 3rd Btn 2nd Marines entered the cove that formed Red Beach 1 they came under murderous fire from in front and from both sides. Within minutes a few amtracs were burning as their unarmored fuel tanks erupted, while others spun out of control as their drivers fell dead or wounded; some just disappeared in a ball of flame as they were blown away by point-blank artillery fire.

Marine Ralph Butler will never forget that day: 'After what seemed like hours of milling about jockeying for positions, we all seemed in proper alignment and proceeded shoreward. Each tractor was equipped with two .50 calibre machine-guns mounted in front and at a certain point the first wave were to start firing. I don't recall how far we were from the shore when all hell let loose; the amtrac started getting hit and our first reaction was that the tractors on our flanks had lost control of their guns.

Another of the amtracs that ended up on the west of Red Beach 1: *My Delores*. Pfc Ed Moore and radio-man Bob Thoreson narrowly escaped when the cab was riddled by machine-gun fire coming through the underside. (USMC)

At the western end of Red Beach 1, amtracs abandoned after the hellish trip ashore on D-day. A dead crew member lies face down in the water near the seawall. (National Archives)

'The sudden realization that there were Japs still alive on the island and capable of resistance snapped everybody out of their joviality. I remember a violent, turbulent trip shoreward, explosions, detonations, bodies slumped and bloody, and finally crunching to a stop. Somebody screamed, "Get the hell out, fast"; throwing equipment out and scrambling over the side onto the beach.'

The fire from the east shore was particularly fierce. Here the enemy had in place 3 inch (75mm) and 1.4 inch (37mm) guns, together with numerous single and twin machine-gun emplacements. This area was destined to be the last part of Betio to be subdued by the Marines. In the face of such heavy fire many amtracs veered away to the west, coming ashore at the junction of Red Beach 1 and Green Beach, where they encountered a 5 foot (1.52m) high seawall, and few Marines could get onto the land.

The first amtrac arrived on the shores of Betio at 0910hrs: No 49 My Delores driven by Pfc Ed Moore. The ride had been hair-raising as they were riddled by machine-gun fire from an emplacement near their landing point at the western end of the beach. Two Marines jumped out and silenced the machine-gun with well-aimed grenades, but another gun sent a hail of bullets into the front of the amtrac, destroying the instrument panel and bringing it to a lurching halt at the water's edge. 'How my radio operator and myself got out of that riddled cab without being hit at the time remains a mystery to me to this day' recalls Moore.

The second and third waves of amtracs suffered even more intense fire, several being shattered by large caliber anti-boat guns, while the survivors scrambled ashore to engage the enemy. Company K was decimated by strongpoints on the eastern shore while Company I lost 50 per cent of its strength in the first half-hour as they made for the western extremity of the beach.

Maj Michael Ryan's L Company were forced to wade ashore when their boats grounded on the reef and suffered 35 per cent casualties: 'As the men struggled ashore I looked for the command elements of the battalion,' he said. 'It never arrived, and I was later informed that the commander believed that our waves were completely destroyed in the water, and he had moved his boat to another beach. After some hours we were convinced that the battalion command was not coming ashore and had probably been destroyed.'

Pfc Bob Libby from the 3.16 inch (81mm) mortar platoon of 3-2 should have been in the third wave of Higgins boats heading for Red 1. The account of his arrival on the beach is an explicit illustration of the horror of Tarawa.

'About 500 yards [455m] out our Higgins boat rammed into the reef, and everyone was ordered over the side. I landed in water well over my head, having missed the reef due to the boat being held up against it. Kicking myself from the bottom, I rose to the surface and found a footing on the reef itself. A quick look round revealed nightmarish activity; I noticed our boat drifting ashore and struck to my right, my intention being to keep the boat between me and the heavy fire coming from shore as long as I could. It was possible to keep a watch for machine gun fire skipping off the surface, a move to one side or the other allowed passage for this while still moving slowly toward the beach. Everywhere and anywhere I looked there were knocked-out amphibious tractors burning fiercely, landing craft being blown apart. The walking wounded were moving in the opposite direction making their way to drifting boats. The water around me was red or pink with a churning mass of spouting geysers; bodies were floating on the surface everywhere I looked; here a man moving along was no longer seen. The sound of screaming shells passed overhead, the unmistakable crack of rifle fire zipped around my ears, the screams of the wounded were almost lost in this cacophony of sound. If anyone can think up a picture of Hell, I don't think that it would match up to that wade-in from the reef to the shore at Tarawa, with floating bodies and bits of bodies, the exploding shells, and burned-out craft; there was no hiding place, no protection: my only armor was the shirt on my back. It took about half an hour from leaving my boat to put foot on dry land.'

RED BEACH 2 – MORNING

In the waters off Red Beach 2 a disaster was brewing. The last of the Marine regiments to land, LtCol Amey's 2nd Btn 2nd Marines, were faced with rows of dug-in enemy emplacements manned by determined *rikusentai* who had had ample time to prepare. The objective was to land F Company on the left, E Company on the right, and for G Company to be in support; but as the first waves of amtracs came within range of the Japanese positions a hail of anti-boat artillery and small-arms fire shredded the water. The coxswains, desperate to escape the blistering barrage, put their vehicles ashore wherever they could find space, and the Marines, many already exhausted and seasick after hours of pitching in the heavy swell, waited helplessly for their craft to make land. As the survivors ground ashore the troops leaped over the sides and headed for the only cover that was available: a log barricade that ran the full length of the beach. As they huddled under their precarious shelter they looked back to see the following waves of Higgins boats already grounding on the reef, and the Marines, burdened with masses of equipment,

AT THE SEAWALL
Major Henry 'Jim' Crowe of the 2nd Battalion 8th Marines was the only Battalion commander to reach the shore on D-day. Major Schoettel failed to land on Red 1 and LtCol Amey died in a hail of machine-gun fire on Red 2. Two of Crowe's amtracs found a gap in the seawall and advanced for 100 yards (91m), but had to return to the beach when the Japanese began filtering between them and the shore, placing the amtracs in danger of being cut off. Here, Major Crowe directs operations from the rear of a grounded amtrac, as his men attempt to advance beyond the seawall.

The seawall, almost the only cover on the beachhead from the accurate Japanese gunfire, it gave the Marines time for a brief respite before they went 'over the top' to attack the airfield. (National Archives)

OPPOSITE *March Macabre* (Kerr Eby). For the Marines lucky enough to survive the landings, the only cover available was the wooden seawall which surrounded a large part of Betio. Casualties among those who attempted to go beyond the wall were catastrophic. (Navy Art Collection, Naval Historical Center)

clambering out and wading inexorably forwards toward entrenched machine guns.

LtCol Amey was only 200 yards (182m) from the beach when his amtrac became entangled in the barbed-wire barricade and would not budge. The colonel and his HQ went over the side and crouched alongside the craft to escape the hail of bullets lashing the water all around them. After a while there was a lull in the fire, and the group headed to the shore on hands and knees to present a smaller target. When the water became too shallow the colonel stood up and shouted: 'Come on – these bastards can't stop us!' and splashed toward the shore: he was hit in the chest and throat by a burst of machine-gun fire and died instantly. With Amey was LtCol Walter Jordan from the 4th Division, who had come along as an observer. As he was the senior officer present he found himself as acting commander of 2-2.

Donald Tyson of the 1st Battalion 18th Marines was assigned to a rifle squad of 2-2. He recalls: 'As we neared the island our machine guns opened up. The blast from our two .50 inch (12.7mm) calibers was ear splitting: the BAR man firing our port-side .50 inch (12.7mm) died instantly as the first rounds of enemy fire raked our amtrac. Simultaneously a steady stream of bullets began coming in one side, and going out the other, with a pinging sound, except where someone's body got in the way. Our starboard-side .50 inch (12.7mm) gunner was killed and a replacement jumped up, grabbed the cocking handle and pulled it back, but was killed before firing a shot. At about this time an anti-boat gun shell tore into our starboard track causing the amtrac to make a half-right turn stop.'

On the left-hand side of the beach F Company lost almost half of its strength as the troops attempted to get to the beach and over the log barrier at the water's edge. Those who made it formed themselves into small units a few yards inland, armed only with light machine guns and other small arms. Most radios were saturated with sea water and were unusable, and runners soon fell prey to enemy snipers

E Company had landed at the junction of Red Beaches 1 and 2 after their amtrac had veered away in the face of heavy mortar and rifle fire. Despite a storm directed at them they succeeded in silencing one Japanese strongpoint, but as the platoon leader fell dead they took cover in a large shell hole.

G Company landed somewhere between the other two, taking heavy losses before they reached the barrier. The beach was already crowded with casualties as men attempted to locate the source of the enemy fire among the mass of palm trees and small huts that stood a little way inland.

OVERLEAF **Wading in. While the amtracs churned over the reef and reached the beachhead, this illustration shows the disastrous results as the Higgins boats grounded on the exposed coral and the Marines were left with no option but to wade ashore. They were faced with murderous artillery, mortar, machine-gun and small arms fire, which accounted for over half of their total casualties. With larger, more heavily armed amtracs for future amphibious operations, the Marines would never again have to face such appalling odds.**

RED BEACH 3 – MORNING

The destroyers *Ringgold* and *Dashiell*, already stationed in the lagoon off Red Beach 3, were an enormous asset to the men of the 2nd Btn 8th Marines. Maintaining a constant barrage of 5 inch (127mm) shells all along the shore they kept the defenders buttoned up long enough for 'Jim' Crowe's team to come ashore with minimal losses, and only 25 casualties in the first wave of LVTs.

Crowe, the only one of the three battalion commanders to get ashore on D-day, had to wade in when his Higgins boat ground to a halt on the reef. Even so he arrived only four minutes behind the last wave of amtracs.

The scheme of maneuver was for E and F Companies to move inland immediately upon landing, while G Company mopped up in their wake; but in the face of devastating fire neither company was going anywhere. A break in the seawall enabled two amtracs to advance as far as the taxiway on the airfield, where they took up a defensive position. However, it was soon apparent that they were outflanked and in danger of being cut off.

The only part of the beachhead where significant gains could be made appeared to be to the east. Here Crowe's executive officer was able

The Hard Road to Triumph **(Kerr Eby) Having survived the shredding enemy fire, the Marines grimly press forward to attack. It is significant that over half of the Marine casualties were incurred during the initial landings and that 75 of the 125 Amphibious Tractors committed to the battle were destroyed on or before reaching the beaches. (Navy Art Collection, Naval Historical Center)**

to push beyond the short pier of the Burns-Philp South Sea Trading Company, but was soon forced back. Crowe responded by sending G Company across their flank, reinforcing it against the counter-attack that he was sure would come at any moment. Like most other regimental commanders that day, he found his radio to be inoperable and sent runners toward the pier in an attempt to make contact with the Marines on Red Beach 2 at his right.

OTHER OPERATIONS

While the three assault regiments were attempting to consolidate their beachheads, Col Shoup was desperate to get ashore. From the mixed reports that he had received it was obvious that things were not going to plan.

His initial attempts to land had been thwarted; he had transferred from a Higgins boat to an amtrac and headed for Red Beach 2, but had to retire under heavy gunfire. An attempt to come in alongside the pier had resulted in his amtrac stalling, and only by transferring to another Higgins boat did the colonel and his HQ finally get ashore around 1030hrs. Sprinting across the beach he received shrapnel wounds in his leg when a mortar shell exploded nearby, but he waived medical help and set up his headquarters at a bunker just inland on Red 2. Communications onshore were proving to be as uncertain as those aboard the *Maryland*. Shoup's attempts to assess the situation were frustrated by the failure of the man-pack radios, most of which had been submerged in seawater during the struggle to get ashore. As they were inoperable, runners were dispatched in an attempt to contact the company commanders to his left and right, but few returned. Gradually however, information did begin to filter through. Shoup became aware that some troops had managed to get ashore on Red 1, and that the battalion commander, Maj Shoettel, was still out in the lagoon. But he did not know that Maj Ryan had landed and was rallying the stragglers at the western end of the beach.

Ryan's battalion commander, Maj Schoettel, had remained out in the lagoon with the fourth wave. Seeing the carnage as the three battalions had entered the cove, he took it upon himself to hold back the fourth and fifth waves in the belief that further landings would be suicide. Around 1000hrs he succeeded in contacting Shoup by radio and sent the message: 'Receiving heavy fire all along beach, unable to land, issue in doubt.' This was followed eight minutes later by: 'Boats held up on reef on right flank Red 1, troops receiving heavy fire in water.' Shoup answered: 'Land Red Beach 2 and work west.' The reply was mystifying: 'We have nothing left to land.'

A little later in the day Schoettel again contacted Shoup to tell him that he had lost contact with his men. Before Shoup could reply, Gen Julian Smith, who had been monitoring the conversation from the *Maryland*, butted in with the terse instruction: 'Direct you land at any cost, regain control of your battalion and continue the attack.'

Maj Schoettel later played a part in silencing the enclave of Japanese fortifications at the junction of Red Beaches 1 and 2 where the enemy made their final stand, but there can be little doubt that his conduct on D-day was less than impressive. After the battle he was transferred to the

22nd Marines and was recommended for a Bronze Star while serving on Eniwetok. He was killed in action on Guam in August 1944.

LtCol Jordan had succeeded in making contact, and was told to retain command of 2-2, most of whom were huddled behind the seawall as Shoup could verify from his command post. On Red 3 he learned that some forward positions were near to the airfield taxiway, and that farther east a few Marines were nearly 200 yards (182m) inland.

Shoup then gave the 1st Btn 2nd Marines, under Maj Wood Kyle, instructions to land on Red 2 and to attempt to work westward to Red 1. However, there was another delay as Kyle searched desperately for enough amtracs to house his Marines. When the battalion finally started for Red 2 they met such a heavy and accurate barrage that many landing craft veered away to the west, ending up at the extremity of Red 1 where they were recruited by Maj Ryan.

Gen Holland Smith had instructed that the 6th Marines were not to be committed without V Corps authority, and they were still aboard the transports off Betio. This left Julian Smith with only the 1st and 3rd Battalions of the 8th Marines in reserve. At 1018hrs Holland Smith decided to send 3-8, under Maj Robert Ruud, to the line of departure so that they would be available to Shoup should he need them.

A Wounded Buddy (Kerr Eby) Corpsmen, the navy medics attached to the Marine Corps, were revered by the Marines. In the thick of the fighting, 'Doc' would be available to treat the most appalling wounds and get the casualties to the nearest doctor or field hospital. (Navy Art Collection, Naval Historical Center)

Maj Michael Ryan, commander of L Company 3-2, who assembled and led a mixed force of Marines on the western side of Red Beach 1. His capture of Green Beach on D+1 proved decisive, allowing the 6th Marines to land on an uncontested beach. (USMC Historical Collection)

Acting upon what information was available to him, Julian Smith radioed Holland Smith, who was with the Northern Task Force off Makin: 'Successful landings on beaches Red 2 and 3. Am committing one landing team from divisional reserves. Still encountering strong resistance throughout.' Holland Smith was perturbed; he knew that it was unusual to commit reserves this early in the battle.

It was at around 1130hrs that Shoup ordered Maj Ruud's 3-8 to land on Red 3 in support of 'Jim' Crowe. There were no amtracs available at the line of departure, and Ruud and his men were left to come ashore the hard way, by Higgins boat.

The Japanese gunners had now worked out the range to perfection, and the first salvos arrived just as the boats reached the reef. As the ramps came down the Marines – most of them laden with heavy equipment – leaped into the water amid a furious barrage from the artillery at the eastern end of Betio. Many disappeared into deep water and drowned; others began the long slog toward the shore amid a criss-cross of machine-gun and small arms fire.

From the shore, Crowe's men could only watch in horror as the ever diminishing figures struggled forward amid exploding landing craft and spouts of artillery fire. LtCdr MacPherson, overhead in his Kingfisher spotter plane, said: 'The water never seemed clear of tiny men, their rifle over their head, slowly wading beachward. I wanted to cry.' Seeing his men facing annihilation, Maj Ruud took the courageous decision to order the fourth wave back. His wisdom was confirmed minutes later when the regimental commander, Col Hall, ordered: 'Land no more troops.'

Julian Smith was now left with only one reserve unit, Maj Lawrence Hays' 1-8, and they were ordered to the line of departure in readiness. At 1330hrs Julian Smith radioed Holland Smith asking V Corps of the 6th Marines to be returned to his command. Permission was granted at 1430hrs, and he now felt confident enough to ask Shoup where he wanted 1-8 to land. His message never got through, so he instructed Hays to land at the extreme eastern end of Betio and work his way northwest to link up with Shoup on Red 2. Yet again the communications foul-up persisted, and this message went missing, with the result that 1-8 spent the remainder of D-day and the whole of the following night embarked in their landing craft and awaiting instructions.

Adm Spruance aboard the *Indianapolis* was short of information, and could see that the operation was faltering. His staff were of the opinion that he should step in and take control, but he declined; he had selected his team and they must be allowed to conduct the battle as they saw fit.

RED BEACH 1 – AFTERNOON

Maj Ryan found himself in charge of a bewildering mixture of men on Red 1. He had the remains of three rifle companies, one machine-gun platoon, plus the remnants of Maj Kyle's 1-2. Over the course of the morning he had also acquired various amtrac drivers, heavy weapons men, engineers, signalers, and corpsmen.

On the eastern side of the cove the formidable cluster of Japanese defenses that had caused such havoc that morning were still intact, and Ryan realized that his best chances lay in attacking south along Green

Beach. He got a message to Shoup at 1415hrs informing him of his situation, and proceeded to carve out a beachhead by overrunning several enemy pill-boxes. However, his big problem was that he had nothing but infantry weapons available to him, and as the afternoon wore on he decided that his best option was to consolidate his position for the night: 'I was convinced that without flame throwers or explosives to clean them out we had to pull back to a perimeter that could be defended against a counter-attack,' he said.

Marines of a .30 (75mm) machine-gun squad work their way inland from cover to cover among a mass of enemy emplacements. This picture illustrates the appalling conditions under which the Marines had to fight – shattered trees, debris, and strength-sapping heat. (National Archives)

RED BEACHES 2 AND 3 – AFTERNOON

By late afternoon of D-day the Marines had a toehold on parts of Red Beaches 2 and 3 that included the area east of the cove on Red 1 up to the Burns-Philp Wharf, with the long pier but casualties had been severe. Shoup instructed Ruud to reorganize his I and L Companies, and as they were so depleted they were absorbed as a composite unit with 'Jim' Crowe's 2-8.

The battleships and cruisers continued to pound the eastern end of the island to prevent reinforcements from moving westward, and the fighters and dive bombers from the carrier support group strafed and

The Marines suffered almost 50 per cent of their casualties during the landings on D-day and D+1. Here, alongside the wooden Japanese latrines, the grim business of identifying the dead gets underway among the bodies washed up on the beaches. (US Navy)

bombed anything that moved outside the Marines' perimeter. Tanks and artillery had been earmarked to play an important role on day one, but due to the chaos on the beaches they were not deployed as planned. LtCol Presley Rixey's 1-10 artillery battalion with their 3 inch (75mm) pack howitzers were still on standby out in the lagoon. It would be much later in the day before Rixey's men could bring some of their weapons ashore by manhandling them to the eastern extremity of Red 2.

Sherman M4-A2 medium tanks with their 3 inch (75mm) main armament had been specially prepared for the landings: 6–8 foot (1.82–2.43m) long extensions were attached to the exhausts and air intakes, to be discarded when they got ashore, and all openings below the anticipated water line were sealed with a tarlike compound. Special reconnaissance platoons had been formed to guide the tank drivers through the mass of shell and bomb craters that would inevitably cover the reef, and bright-orange floats were prepared to mark the corridors through which they would pass. Melvin Swango was a member of one of these platoons on Red Beach 2: 'In the 700–800 yards [637–726m] between the edge of the reef and the beach we would attempt to plot a safe route for the tanks. It was an awesome responsibility.' Many of his group were killed or wounded as their landing craft reached the edge of the reef, the remainder plunged over the side into shoulder-deep water and began their hazardous task.

'From the beginning it was apparent that the floats were not going to work, the ropes became soggy with salt water and could not be separated from each other, and the anchors were too light to hold the floats in place. We spread out in a single line, spacing ourselves as far apart as possible while still being able to see any crater that might appear **45**

THE MARINES ATTACK, NOVEMBER 20 1943

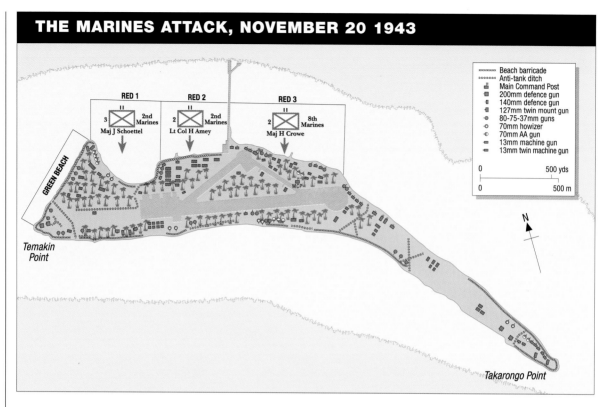

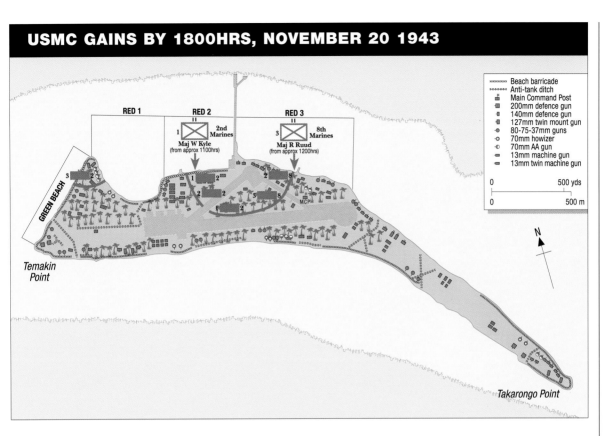

RED 1

RED 2

RED 3

2nd
Marines
1
Maj W Kyle
(from approx 1100hrs)

8th
Marines
3
Maj R Ruud
(from approx 1200hrs)

GREEN BEACH

Temakin
Point

MCP

Takarongo Point

N

xxxxxxxxx	Beach barricade
>>>>>>>	Anti-tank ditch
	Main Command Post
	200mm defence gun
	140mm defence gun
	127mm twin mount gun
	80-75-37mm guns
	70mm howizer
	70mm AA gun
	13mm machine gun
	13mm twin machine gun

0   500 yds

0   500 m

BELOW, LEFT Lt Rudloff's Sherman tank was hit several times by Japanese missiles during the battle on Betio but remained in action. (National Archives)

between us. At each crater one man would remain to wave the tanks safely by. The closer we approached the island the more intense became the enemy fire: grimly I observed that each time I surveyed our little group there were fewer of us.

'Our tanks watched for us as they plowed through the water, exhausts roaring like some terrible denizens from the deep. Occasionally one of the tank hatches would tilt slightly, and one of our buddies would wave a friendly salute. Finally all the tanks had passed – most of them made it – a few met with mishaps and drowned-out or were abandoned. I looked about for other members of our group but only a handful were left.'

Eight tanks from C Company's 2nd and 3rd platoons had attempted the landing on Red 3; one flooded-out, but the remainder got ashore, and Maj Crowe directed them east in support of his infantry.

On Red Beach 1, six Shermans had made a landing but four flooded-out or became bogged down in shell-holes; the two that successfully made it to the beach, *Chicago* and *China Gal*, were forced to take an indirect and torturous route inland to avoid the scores of Marine casualties on the narrow beach. *Chicago* was knocked-out by the enemy artillery fire, but *China Gal* made its way to Green Beach and became a valuable addition to Maj Ryan's force—albeit with her main 3 inch (75mm) gun inoperable.

The confusion at command level gradually worsened and to try to clarify the situation ashore Julian Smith sent his second in command, BrigGen Leo Hermle, to land on the pier, collect information and report back. Hermle was unable to locate Shoup's HQ and when he tried to contact Smith later in the day he could not reach him. Hermle stayed on

the pier until D+1 and then returned to the *Maryland* only to discover that Smith had sent him a message which he never got, ordering him to take command on the island. The end result was that David Shoup remained in command on Betio on D+1.

Coming ashore after his grueling task of guiding the waterproofed Shermans through the shell-holes to Red Beach 2, Melvin Swango (left), his hand bandaged from lacerations and burns received earlier in the day, dodges around the plethora of abandoned gear on the beachhead. (USMC)

THE DEFENDERS

Although Adm Shibasaki's boast that the Marines could not take Tarawa with 'a million men in a thousand years' was pure hyperbole, the *rikusentai* put up a fiercely determined defense. Their well-coordinated and accurate fire, particularly from Red Beaches 1 and 2, had caused grievous casualties to the initial row of amtracs, and the Marines, who had been compelled to wade ashore from their LCVP Higgins boats when they ground to a halt on the reef, had been decimated.

The admiral's four months of intensive training was paying off, although he would no doubt have regretted that he had concentrated on the southern and western defenses, anticipating that these were the most likely site for the American landings. His ambition to encircle the islands with mines, tetrahedrons, and barricades had also been thwarted by lack of time. The 3,000 mines that remained in storage were a reminder that the reefs could have been an even more formidable barrier to the invaders.

It was sometime on the afternoon of D-day that an incident was to occur that would irrevocably alter the course of the battle in favor of the Americans. A sharp-eyed Marine somewhere on the island spotted a

The Japanese caused devastating damage to the amtracs approaching Red Beach 1. Here abandoned LVTs and floating bodies at the log barricade bear witness to the effectiveness of the defenses. (National Archives)

group of Japanese officers standing in the open and called in naval gunfire from the *Ringgold* and *Dashiell* who obliged with a salvo of 5 inch (127mm) rounds fuzed as air bursts. The group turned out to be Adm Shibasaki and his entire staff. In a gesture of benevolence, they had decided to give up their concrete blockhouse HQ for use as a hospital, and to move to a secondary command post a few hundred yards away. The resultant explosion killed Shibasaki and his entire staff.

The importance of Shibasaki's death cannot be overestimated; had he lived he would doubtless have launched a massive counter-attack on the night of D-day against the precariously positioned Marines. There were scarcely 3,000 ashore, clinging to isolated pockets no more than a few yards inland, with little artillery support and few tanks. The Japanese were known to excel in night-time fighting, while the Marines favored defensive positions at night. What would have happened had this attack occurred is open to speculation: at best the Marines would have been subjected to a massive assault along the length of their front, with the inevitable huge casualties; at worst it could have been a monumental disaster.

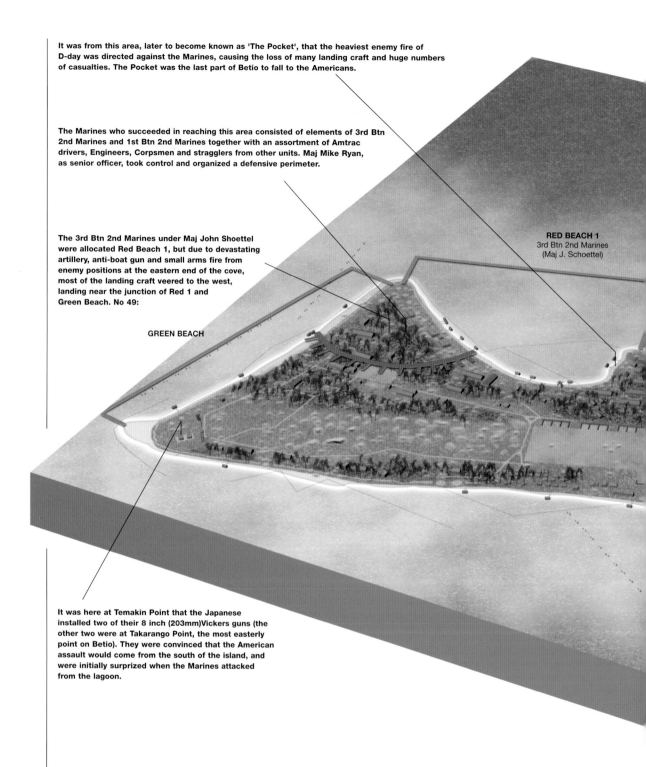

It was from this area, later to become known as 'The Pocket', that the heaviest enemy fire of D-day was directed against the Marines, causing the loss of many landing craft and huge numbers of casualties. The Pocket was the last part of Betio to fall to the Americans.

The Marines who succeeded in reaching this area consisted of elements of 3rd Btn 2nd Marines and 1st Btn 2nd Marines together with an assortment of Amtrac drivers, Engineers, Corpsmen and stragglers from other units. Maj Mike Ryan, as senior officer, took control and organized a defensive perimeter.

The 3rd Btn 2nd Marines under Maj John Shoettel were allocated Red Beach 1, but due to devastating artillery, anti-boat gun and small arms fire from enemy positions at the eastern end of the cove, most of the landing craft veered to the west, landing near the junction of Red 1 and Green Beach. No 49:

RED BEACH 1
3rd Btn 2nd Marines
(Maj J. Schoettel)

GREEN BEACH

It was here at Temakin Point that the Japanese installed two of their 8 inch (203mm)Vickers guns (the other two were at Takarango Point, the most easterly point on Betio). They were convinced that the American assault would come from the south of the island, and were initially surprized when the Marines attacked from the lagoon.

BETIO ISLAND, TARAWA ATOLL
D-DAY NOVEMBER 20, 1943
USMC approximate gains by 1800hrs

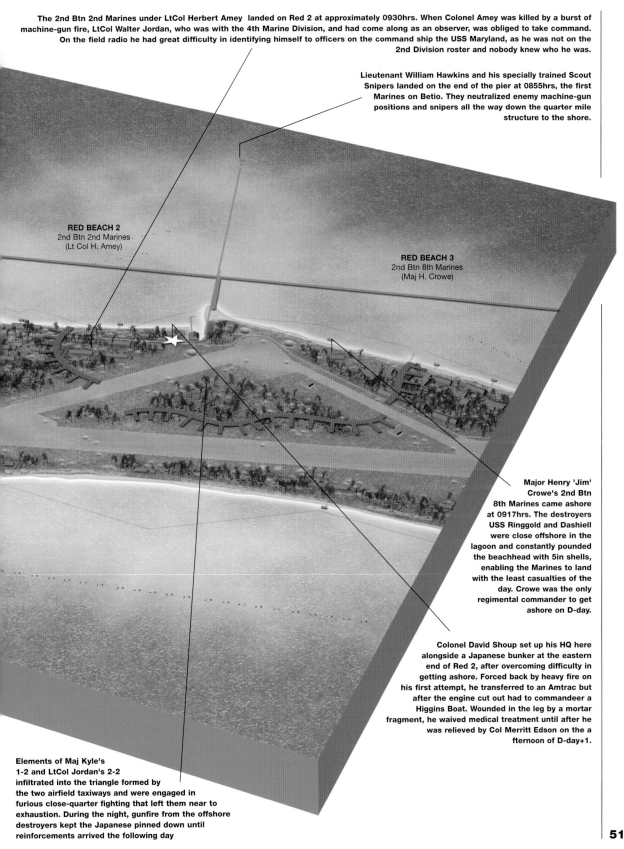

The 2nd Btn 2nd Marines under LtCol Herbert Amey landed on Red 2 at approximately 0930hrs. When Colonel Amey was killed by a burst of machine-gun fire, LtCol Walter Jordan, who was with the 4th Marine Division, and had come along as an observer, was obliged to take command. On the field radio he had great difficulty in identifying himself to officers on the command ship the USS Maryland, as he was not on the 2nd Division roster and nobody knew who he was.

Lieutenant William Hawkins and his specially trained Scout Snipers landed on the end of the pier at 0855hrs, the first Marines on Betio. They neutralized enemy machine-gun positions and snipers all the way down the quarter mile structure to the shore.

RED BEACH 2
2nd Btn 2nd Marines
(Lt Col H. Amey)

RED BEACH 3
2nd Btn 8th Marines
(Maj H. Crowe)

Major Henry 'Jim' Crowe's 2nd Btn 8th Marines came ashore at 0917hrs. The destroyers USS Ringgold and Dashiell were close offshore in the lagoon and constantly pounded the beachhead with 5in shells, enabling the Marines to land with the least casualties of the day. Crowe was the only regimental commander to get ashore on D-day.

Colonel David Shoup set up his HQ here alongside a Japanese bunker at the eastern end of Red 2, after overcoming difficulty in getting ashore. Forced back by heavy fire on his first attempt, he transferred to an Amtrac but after the engine cut out had to commandeer a Higgins Boat. Wounded in the leg by a mortar fragment, he waived medical treatment until after he was relieved by Col Merritt Edson on the afternoon of D-day+1.

Elements of Maj Kyle's 1-2 and LtCol Jordan's 2-2 infiltrated into the triangle formed by the two airfield taxiways and were engaged in furious close-quarter fighting that left them near to exhaustion. During the night, gunfire from the offshore destroyers kept the Japanese pinned down until reinforcements arrived the following day

D-DAY+1

The American foothold on Betio was tenuous. On the right of Red Beach 1, Maj Ryan and his assorted band held a strip of the island about 250 yards (228m) wide and 300 yards (273m) long, with the sea on both sides. They were short of supplies and had no means of evacuation.

On the combined Red 2 and 3 beachheads the troops were in sporadic contact with each other but there was a 600 yard (546m) gap between them and Ryan. Their line ended 300 yards (273m) from the main pier, and to the east, near the Burns-Philp wharf, a few Marines had forced their way inland to within yards of the main runway of the airfield.

Shoup was sure that there would be a major counter-attack that night, and Gen Julian Smith was to spend what he later admitted were the worst hours of his military career there: 'Hold what you have, develop contact between landing teams, make provision to meet organized counter-attack,' he signaled to Shoup's HQ.

The Americans were unaware of the death of Shibasaki: for decades it was assumed that he died sometime near the end of the battle. The absence of the anticipated attack was a puzzle to the staff of V Corps. Tenacious and fearless fighters that they were, it was a curious fact that, once deprived of leadership, the Japanese soldier soon became disorganized and disillusioned. They lacked the Marines' ability to re-group with other unfamiliar units, or to act individually.

There was some sporadic fire from the Japanese lines during the early hours, and aircraft from the Marshall Islands made an unsuccessful

Admiral Shibasaki's concrete bunker. It was here, on D-day, that the Admiral and his entire HQ staff were killed by naval gunfire. This photo, taken after the battle, shows an abandoned Type 95 tank and indicates the terrific pounding that the structure suffered during the course of the battle. (USMC)

Somewhere on the invasion
beaches a group of Marines are
pinned down. Shallow advances
were made here and there by
small and uncoordinated groups
like this one but it was not until
D+1 that significant movement
inland was achieved.
(National Archives)

attempt to bomb shipping to the west of the island, but on the whole the
night was fairly uneventful. With daylight came the heat, and all over the
northern half of Betio Marines became aware of an awful smell. The
scores of bodies littering the beaches and shoreline were starting to
decompose where they lay; the area was still far too dangerous for the
burial parties to move in, and the stench would become one of the
battle's enduring memories for the Marines as the death toll reached the
thousands over the next two days.

Maj Hays' 1-8 were still embarked in their Higgins boats at the line of
departure. Having spent almost 24 hours without food, drink or toilet
facilities they were not in the best of moods. At 0615hrs they were finally
ordered to head for Red 2, and as the Higgins boats again grounded on
the reef the Japanese laid on a barrage of murderous machine gun and
rifle fire: it was obvious that nothing had been learned from the previous
day.

Just after Hays' men hit the reef, two navy lieutenants, John Fletcher
and Eddie A. Heimberger, from the transport *Sheridan*, became aware
that up to 150 wounded Marines were stranded on the reef. Working
independently they began rescuing the men and taking them out to tank
lighters offshore for transportation to hospital ships. The propeller on
Heimberger's craft was seriously damaged on the coral and he limped
back to the lagoon and commandeered a LCVP, returning to collect

ABOVE **All along the beaches the bodies of Marines killed on D-day create a dreadful flotsam. Here on Red Beach 1 near a swamped-out tank, the pathetic figures await collection and identification by the war graves teams. (National Archives)**

RIGHT **The same scene from the opposite direction. (National Archives)**

more injured Marines. By now the tide was rapidly going in and he was subjected to heavy enemy fire.

Realizing that he was making little impact with only one boat, Heimberger rounded up several other LCVPs and again approached the reef. This time he came under fire from both the shore batteries and from the *Niminoa*: the old wreck lying west of the main pier. He returned fire with the .30 calibre machine guns which were part of the LCVPs armament, and signalled his other boats to stay 200 yards (182m) from the reef while he went out to duel with the Japanese in the *Niminoa*. Working his way back to the reef, he again came under fire from a lone Japanese sniper who had swum out to a wrecked LCVP. Aware that he was carrying eight drums of high octane fuel, he rapidly disposed of the sniper before resuming his task of collecting the wounded.

During the afternoon he took on board 13 Marines. Thirty-five others who were not wounded asked him to bring them weapons to replace the ones that had been lost in the water; he said he would try and backed off. Heimberger later met Col Hall, commanding officer of the 8th Marines, who was making his way to the beach, and informed him of the snipers aboard the *Niminoa* and the stranded Marines on the reef. Hall gave instructions to his regimental surgeon to board Heimberger's boat to do what he could for the wounded.

The young lieutenant was to receive the Navy Cross for his actions that day, and after the war resumed his career as an actor working professionally under his Christian and middle names: Eddie Albert. It is ironic that in the film for which he is best remembered: *Attack!*, he won acclaim portraying a cowardly officer.

Shoup later called a temporary halt to the landings while Hellcat fighter-bombers attacked the *Niminoa* with 500 lb (225kg) bombs and

Bullets and Barbed Wire
(Kerr Eby)
No amphibious landing in the whole of the Pacific War presented the Marines with such horrendous obstacles. Grounding on the reefs, the Marines were left with no option but to wade to the beach in the face of murderous enemy fire.
(Navy Art Collection, Naval Historical Center)

machine-gun fire but the attack had little effect and only one bomb hit the ship. Eventually it was left to the guns of the *Maryland* and *Colorado* to reduce the hulk to a mangled heap of metal.

Col Rixey had brought some of his artillery ashore the previous night and now it was brought into action. Siting two of his (75mm) pack howitzers at the eastern end of Red 2 he began pounding the strongpoints at the end of the cove, enabling Hays' 1-8 to get ashore with a few less casualties.

At 0800hrs Hays reported to Shoup with what remained of his battalion; casualties were around 50 per cent, and a great deal of equipment had been lost in the water. As the day wore on and the tide rose, a flow of heavier equipment such as 1.44 inch (37mm) anti-tank guns, jeeps, bulldozers, and half-tracks would get ashore, but for the moment Shoup would have to make do with what he had.

The principal objective for D+1 was to reach the far side of Betio, cutting the Japanese garrison in two, and to link up with Maj Ryan. His surviving Marines were sent to bolster the troops on the right flank of Red 2, but even with the help of a tank to beef-up the attack, little headway was made and a grim stalemate set in.

The Japanese had used the first night to consolidate their inland defenses. The Marines who had succeeded in crossing the western taxiway of the airfield on D-day were now trapped in a 'triangle' formed by the taxiways and the main runway. The Japanese had set machine guns to cover this area; anyone attempting to cross them faced almost certain death. The Marines in the 'triangle' – mainly Companies A and B of Wood Kyle's 1-2 – were virtually cut off from Red Beach 2. Shoup was determined to get his men across Betio, and after a concerted bombardment by carrier planes, these Marines raced across the 125 yard (114m) strip between the 'triangle' and the sea, occupied a 200 yard

OPPOSITE, TOP **Moving across the island was a precarious business. Here Marines dash across open ground from one position to another. Japanese machine guns set up to enfilade the area around the airfield taxiways occupied by scattered groups from the 2nd and 8th Marines made movement especially perilous. (National Archives)**

OPPOSITE, BOTTOM **Occupying the wreckage of a Japanese emplacement, Marines fend off counter-attacks. While one marine throws a hand grenade, the other has a brief respite, taking a drink from his near empty canteen. (National Archives)**

BELOW **One of the .30 inch (75mm) pack howitzers of Col Rixey's 10th Marines in action. The section commander, standing in the center, is identified as Sgt Armstrong – note the entry and exit holes of a bullet or splinter in his helmet. (USMC)**

On Makin Island, a wounded
soldier is tended by medics of
the 2nd Btn 165th Infantry
Regiment. (National Archives)

(182m) long trench, and dug in. The enemy mounted a vicious counter-attack from the eastern flank, and the Marines suffered heavy casualties before a temporary lull set in.

Later in the afternoon, Shoup sent Col Jordan and his 2-2 command over to the south side where Jordan assumed command. It had been hoped that this combined group would have been able to strike past and link up with Crowe, who was pressing inland from Red 3, but Jordan radioed back that he had fewer than 200 men, including 30 wounded, and that ammunition, grenades, food, and water were in very short supply. Given the circumstances, Shoup told him to consolidate his position and he would endeavor to send supplies across by amtrac.

The attempts to break out of Red Beach 3 by Crowe and his men were being frustrated by a complex of pill-boxes and a large bombproof shelter just beyond the Burns-Philp wharf. The exchanges of fire continued for most of the day, and scores of the enemy were killed, but there seemed to be a never-ending supply of reinforcements. 'Where the hell are they coming from?' fumed Crowe. 'Do they have a tunnel to Tokyo or something?'

Meanwhile, over on Green Beach, the most significant gains of D+1 (and probably of the whole battle) were being made by Maj Ryan and his assortment of Marines. Bolstered by the arrival of *China Gal* – minus her .3 inch (75mm) gun, but still valuable as a mobile machine-gun platform – and *Cecilia*, another Sherman that had bogged down on D-day but had now been recovered, Ryan was preparing to advance along the length of Green Beach to Temakin Point, the southwest extremity of Betio.

Green Beach after the landing of Maj Jones' 1-6 on D+1. The collection of rubber boats lie abandoned on the shore, and a few amtracs are at the water's edge. Nearby troops assemble on the beaches. (US Navy)

During the night a naval gunfire spotter, Lt Thomas Green, had come ashore and was in contact with two offshore destroyers. At 1000hrs a bombardment of the enemy emplacements all along the beach got under way. 'The attack that morning was well coordinated,' said Ryan. 'In fact, the fire requested was so close to where we reported our front line that the naval ships would not respond to the request unless the divisional commander himself approved.'

When the barrage lifted, the Marines swept forward with *Cecilia* clearing the way for the infantry, and by 1100hrs the advance party were standing alongside the 8 inch (203mm) Vickers guns at Temakin Point. In one short and brilliantly coordinated attack Ryan had cleared Green Beach, leaving it open for the 6th Marines to make their much delayed landing. It is little wonder that Julian Smith would declare it 'the most cheering news of D+1.' Ryan was soon to advise Shoup that he was regrouping his force for a thrust eastward across Red Beach 1, but when the message came back from HQ to stay where he was, he deployed his force to consolidate his gains.

At 1600hrs on D+1 Col Shoup gave Julian Smith an assessment of the situation on Betio. Ryan and his group held Green Beach to a depth of 100–150 yards (0.91–137m); on Red 2 the elements of 1-8 held the beach as far as the Japanese strongpoint at the edge of the cove; and 3-8 were deployed near the Burns-Philp wharf on Red 3. Inland, 2-8 had pushed forward to the edge of the airfield's main runway, and on the south coast

With the beachhead secure it was possible to unload the supplies so desperately needed by the Marines. Here an LVT stands with its doors open as a tractor hauls out large boxes. (National Archives).

parts of 1-2 and 2-2 had a 200 yard (182m) enclave, with the enemy to their east and west. He added: 'Casualties many, percentage dead not known, combat efficiency—we are winning.' The way was now open for unopposed landings on Green Beach, and the transport *Feland* closed to within 1,200 yards (1,092m) of the shore; so secure was the beach that Maj William Jones' 1st Btn 6th Marines came ashore in rubber boats (LCRs) usually used for river crossings. However, they did not prove to be suitable for this type of operation, and many had to be taken in tow by Higgins boats. Because of these and other delays, the landing was not completed until 1900hrs, and many of the 2nd Battalion tanks came ashore in darkness. Consequently 1-6 stayed on Green Beach for the night and prepared themselves for the attack the following morning.

Sometime during the afternoon of D+1 an observer on one of the warships in the lagoon reported seeing Japanese troops moving from Betio to Bairiki, the next island in the group. (At low tide it was possible to wade or swim across the coral strip which connected the islands.) Col Raymond Murray's 2-6, who were to have supported Jones' 1-6, were now diverted to block this escape route.

The end of D+1 saw the Marines in a much more favorable position. The failure of the enemy to counter-attack on day one had given the Americans the advantage, and from there onward the issue was not in doubt. Supplies were streaming down the long pier, Col Rixey had been able to get the remainder of his artillery ashore, and at 2030hrs Col Merritt Edson, the divisional chief-of-staff, arrived to take over command from the almost exhausted Shoup. Although Edson was to officially take over on Betio, Col Shoup remained ashore until the end of the battle and, after having his now infected leg wounds treated, continued as Edson's assistant.

War correspondent Robert Sherrod had arrived on the afternoon of D-Day after a 700 yard (640m) wade ashore, during which he faced the full fury of the Japanese barrage. During his trip he had been amazed to see an almost naked Japanese appear from under the water and climb into an abandoned tank. He reported the incident when he got ashore, but the Marine officer was obviously too preoccupied to do anything about it. Sherrod, who wrote a fine book about the battle a few months after his return to America in 1944, reported many memorable sights during the battle: 'I found myself a "safe" spot behind a disabled amtrac near the sea wall; not 15 minutes later I saw the most gruesome sight that I had so far seen in this war.

'A young Marine walked along the beach; he grinned at a pal who was sitting next to me. There was a shot and the Marine spun all the way around and fell to the ground dead. From where he lay a few feet away, he looked at us. Because he had been shot square through the temple, his eyes bulged out wide as if in horrific surprise at what had happened to him.'

From somewhere on the island a last message was flashed to Tokyo: 'Our weapons have been destroyed. From now on everyone is attempting a final charge; may Japan exist for ten thousand years.'

D-DAY+2

For the third day of the battle Edson and Shoup decided on a three-front attack. Jones' 1-6 were to pass through Ryan's men and attack eastward, between the southern limit of the airfield and the sea, to link up with elements of 1-2 and 2-2 on the southern shore. At the same time Maj Hays' 1-8 were to strike west from their positions on Red 2 in an effort to reduce the stubborn pocket of gun emplacements at the junction of Red 1 and 2. The third phase was to be an eastward thrust against the enemy inland from the Burn-Philp wharf by Col Elmer Hall's 2-8 and 3-8 Marines. It was a bold plan, especially considering that only Jones' men were fresh; the others had been fighting ceaselessly for two days and nights with limited supplies of water, and little food.

Meanwhile, LtCol Kenneth McLeod and the Marines of 3-6, who had been kept in readiness at the point of departure since 1600hrs the previous day by a series of contradictory instructions, finally came ashore on Green Beach at 0800hrs, much to their relief.

Just after 0800hrs, Jones and his 1-6 got underway. Because of the narrowness of their front – less than 100 yards (0.91m) – they were forced to advance in columns of companies, spearheaded by three light tanks, with C Company in the lead. Enemy opposition was surprisingly light, and the column reached the enclave on the south shore at 1100hrs having covered the 1,000 yards (910m) in less than three hours, a quite sensational advance by the standards of the previous days.

After a brief stop, Jones pressed on eastward, and with the help of naval gunfire and an air strike by Hellcat fighters, cleared a cluster of pill-boxes and bunkers, inflicting a further 100 casualties on the enemy.

Maj Hays' men of 1-8 began their assault on the formidable stronghold at Red 1-2 at 0700hrs with C Company inland, A Company in the center, and B Company near the beach. Three M3A1 light tanks (Stuarts) spearheaded the assault, but the Marines had only advanced 100 yards (0.91m) when they met stiff opposition from a complex of pill-boxes constructed of palm logs and covered in sand, all with

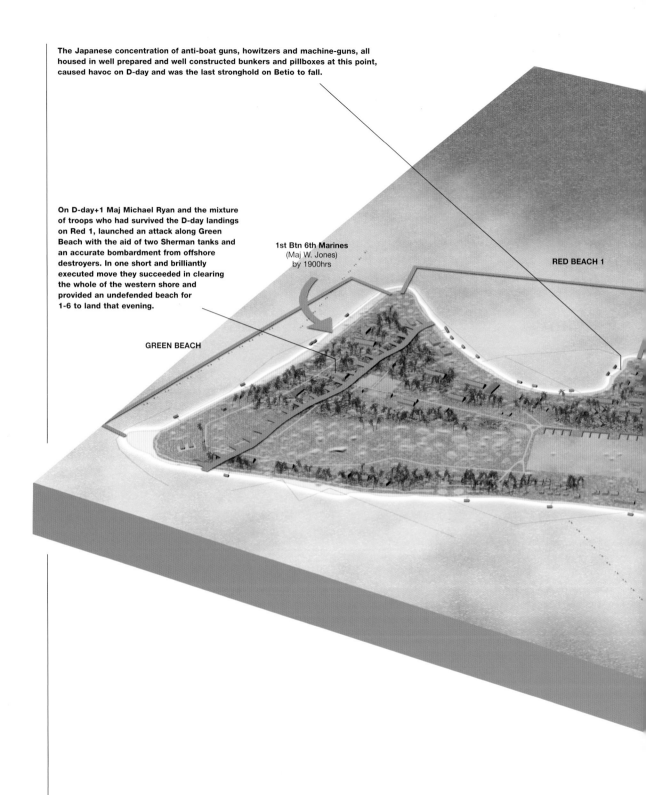

The Japanese concentration of anti-boat guns, howitzers and machine-guns, all housed in well prepared and well constructed bunkers and pillboxes at this point, caused havoc on D-day and was the last stronghold on Betio to fall.

On D-day+1 Maj Michael Ryan and the mixture of troops who had survived the D-day landings on Red 1, launched an attack along Green Beach with the aid of two Sherman tanks and an accurate bombardment from offshore destroyers. In one short and brilliantly executed move they succeeded in clearing the whole of the western shore and provided an undefended beach for 1-6 to land that evening.

1st Btn 6th Marines
(Maj W. Jones)
by 1900hrs

RED BEACH 1

GREEN BEACH

BETIO ISLAND, TARAWA ATOLL
D-DAY+1, NOVEMBER 21, 1943

USMC approximate gains by 1800hrs

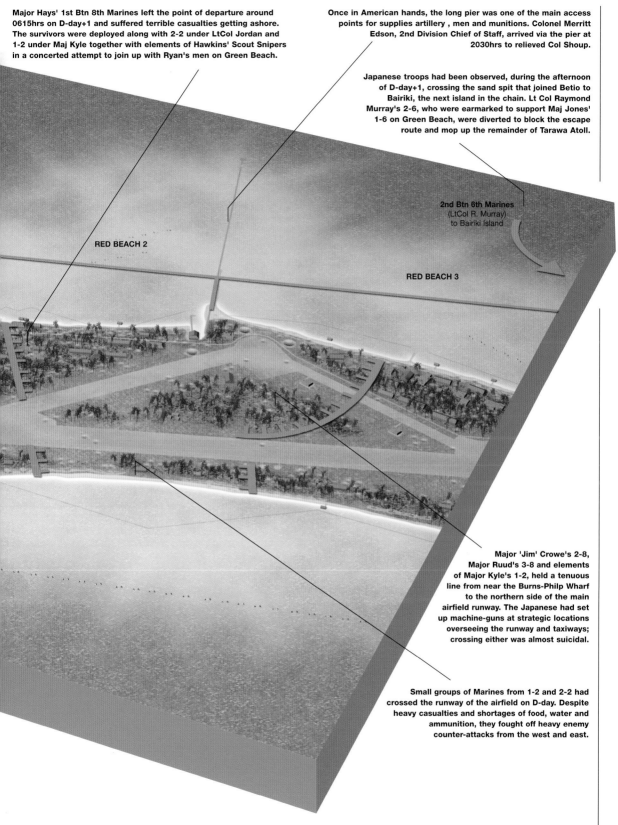

Major Hays' 1st Btn 8th Marines left the point of departure around 0615hrs on D-day+1 and suffered terrible casualties getting ashore. The survivors were deployed along with 2-2 under LtCol Jordan and 1-2 under Maj Kyle together with elements of Hawkins' Scout Snipers in a concerted attempt to join up with Ryan's men on Green Beach.

Once in American hands, the long pier was one of the main access points for supplies artillery , men and munitions. Colonel Merritt Edson, 2nd Division Chief of Staff, arrived via the pier at 2030hrs to relieved Col Shoup.

Japanese troops had been observed, during the afternoon of D-day+1, crossing the sand spit that joined Betio to Bairiki, the next island in the chain. Lt Col Raymond Murray's 2-6, who were earmarked to support Maj Jones' 1-6 on Green Beach, were diverted to block the escape route and mop up the remainder of Tarawa Atoll.

2nd Btn 6th Marines
(LtCol R. Murray)
to Bairiki Island

RED BEACH 2

RED BEACH 3

Major 'Jim' Crowe's 2-8, Major Ruud's 3-8 and elements of Major Kyle's 1-2, held a tenuous line from near the Burns-Philp Wharf to the northern side of the main airfield runway. The Japanese had set up machine-guns at strategic locations overseeing the runway and taxiways; crossing either was almost suicidal.

Small groups of Marines from 1-2 and 2-2 had crossed the runway of the airfield on D-day. Despite heavy casualties and shortages of food, water and ammunition, they fought off heavy enemy counter-attacks from the west and east.

Advancing against a complex of enemy strongholds the Marines could find little shelter amid the shattered trees. Most veterans recall that merely lying down on the sands of Betio was unbearably hot. (National Archives)

mutually supporting fields of fire. The Stuart tanks attempted to reduce these obstructions, but their tiny 1.4 inch (37mm) guns did not pack a big enough punch to cause any serious damage, and they were replaced by two SPMs – 3 inch (75mm) guns mounted on M3 half-tracks from the special weapons battalion. These guns were more effective, and some of the positions were leveled, but the thinly armored half-tracks proved to be vulnerable to enemy fire and had to be withdrawn. By the end of the day the 'Pocket,' as it became known, had not been cleared as Edson and Shoup had hoped. In fact this would remain the last position on Betio to fall to the Americans.

Maj 'Jim' Crowe's composite unit from 2-8 and 3-8 was to advance eastward, pushing beyond the Burn-Philp wharf and toward the eastern end of the main runway. They soon came upon three major obstacles: a steel pillbox; a coconut log machine-gun emplacement; and a large concrete shelter. All three were mutually supporting: an attack on any one and the Marines would immediately come under fire from the other two. Starting with a mortar barrage the Marines struck lucky: one round landed in a heap of ammunition in the log emplacement causing the whole position to erupt in flames, dirt, and cartwheeling timber. A Sherman tank assaulted the pillbox at point-blank range, and engineers finished it off with grenades and TNT charges.

This was the kind of terrain over which Jones' 1-6 had to advance on D+1. Defoliated palm trees, massive shell-holes filled with water, and dozens of wooden structures create a lunar landscape. (National Archives)

The concrete shelter proved to be a tougher nut to crack. For an hour assault engineers, with demolition charges and flame-throwers, fought for control of the structure, finally dropping grenades down the vertical ventilator pipes and flushing out swarms of Japanese soldiers, who were then decimated by canister shot from nearby Stuart tanks. It was as a result of this particular operation that Lt Alexander Bonnyman was to receive a posthumous Medal of Honor.

With these obstacles cleared, Crowe's men surged forward to the end of the runway, where they joined the left flank of Jones' column. Apart from the 'Pocket,' and a few isolated groups of enemy troops, the Marines (to all intents and purposes) held the western two-thirds of Betio. Gen Julian Smith had come ashore during the morning on Green Beach, and after a brief inspection transferred to the command post of Red 2 to join Edson and Shoup.

The smell of death hung heavily over the island. Hundreds of bodies lay where they had fallen; blasted, torn, burned, and swollen, they presented a grotesque sight. Out in the lagoon the bodies of Marines who had died on the first two days bobbed back-and-forth on the tide, bloated, and decomposing in the sweltering heat. Attempts were made to clear the corpses away. Marines were buried in temporary graves while the Japanese were disposed of in a less ceremonious manner: bulldozed into trenches or shell-holes, or loaded onto landing craft on the south shore and dumped at sea.

The Marines also came across significant numbers of Japanese who had obviously killed themselves. Seeing that defeat was inevitable, they were returning to their bunkers and shooting themselves, the favored method being to place the rifle muzzle under the chin and press the trigger with the big toe.

RIGHT **One of the burial parties whose unpleasant duty was to deal with the countless decomposing bodies. (USMC)**

BELOW **Marines, probably from 'Jim' Crowe's 2-8 and 3-8 battle for the sand-covered bunker behind Red Beach 3 which was neutralized largely due to the heroism of Lt Alexander Bonnyman. (US Navy)**

LEFT AND BELOW **Even after D-day, bodies remained unburied on the beaches and around pill-boxes and log emplacements all over the island. It was scenes such as this, authorized for publication by President Roosevelt, that brought the horror of total war home to the American public. (Left – US Navy. Below – National Archives).**

Sensing the inevitability of defeat, many Japanese killed themselves rather than face the dishonor of surrender. Here one has shot himself, his toe is still on the trigger of his rifle, while another chooses death in the open. (Left – National Archives. Below left – USMC).

At around 1930hrs that night about 50 Japanese quietly crept out of the undergrowth and began probing the front of 1-6's defenses. Jones moved up a group from his HQ company along with a mortar platoon, and soon a fierce hand-to-hand fight, with knives and bayonets, developed; after about an hour the enemy retired.

At 0300hrs a second, and much larger, assault was mounted. Screaming *rikusentai* charged out of the brush, hurling grenades and wildly firing their rifles. Shouts of 'Marines you die!' and 'Japanese drink marine blood!' filled the air as several hundred charged across the battalion front. This was the famous 'banzai' charge that was soon to become familiar to Marines throughout the Pacific theater. The guns of the destroyers *Schroeder* and *Sigsbee* were called in to blast the area east of the airfield in order to prevent reinforcements moving up, while the Marines dealt with a nightmare of stabbing, chopping, and desperate clawing with bare hands as the enemy came hurtling out of the darkness.

Dawn revealed the extent of the carnage. Immediately in front of 1-6's positions over 200 Japanese lay dead, and beyond them a further 125 lay mangled by naval gunfire. Jones' men suffered 173 casualties, 45 dead, and the remainder wounded. The enemy's great banzai had failed – for the Japanese left on Betio there was little hope.

D-DAY+3

As November 23 dawned on a corpse-strewn landscape of shredded palm trees, shell-holes, and smashed pill-boxes, Kenneth McLeod's 3-6 passed through Jones' battalion, and the grizzly remains of the failed night-time banzai charge, to press forwards toward the 'tail' of the island to engage the remaining Betio garrison.

Destroyers and carrier planes had battered the area from 0700hrs to 0730hrs, and at 0800hrs McLeod moved out on a 300 yard (273m) front. Company L on the left and Company I on the right were supported by two Shermans and seven Stuart tanks; ahead lay a maze of dug-outs, blockhouses, and log emplacements manned by an estimated 500 Japanese soldiers, for whom surrender was not an option.

There was little resistance until the troops got beyond the anti-tank ditch that ran most of the way across the island, some 100 yards (0.91m) past the end of the airfield runway. Here a complex of pillboxes and trenches barred the way, and not wishing to lose the impetus of the advance, McLeod bypassed this area with L Company leaving I Company and a few tanks to mop up.

A group of Marines check out an enemy dugout of the type that McLeod's men encountered as they advanced along the 'tail' of Betio. The camouflaged jackets and helmet covers were typical of this period, and the standard '782 gear' has been discarded in favor of just rifles and grenades. (National Archives)

The eastern end of Betio, a mass of shell craters, both on land and on the reef. In the foreground a tank trap stretches from shore to shore with another further down the island. McLeod's men killed nearly 500 of the enemy in this area. (US Navy).

At one blockhouse the enemy came charging out en masse and a point-blank 3 inch (75mm) high-explosive round from a Sherman accounted for an estimated 50–75 Japanese. Between here and Takarongo Point (about 1,400 yards; 1,274m) the Marines accounted for some 475 of the enemy for the loss of only 9 killed and 25 wounded. At 1300hrs a sweaty Marine stepped onto the sand spit at the far tip of Betio and swilled the dust from his face; the whole eastern half of the island was in American hands.

'At no time was there any determined defense. I did not use artillery at all and called for naval gunfire for only about five minutes. We used flamethrowers and could have used more. Medium tanks were excellent; my light tanks didn't fire a shot' says McLeod. By the morning of November 23, the only sizeable body of the enemy were the defenders of the Pocket; the determined gun crews holed up in their formidable emplacements at the boundary of Red Beaches 1 and 2.

They had already survived three days of fierce attacks and had undoubtedly been responsible for more Marine casualties than any other group of Japanese defenders. Shoup's plan called for Hays' 1-8 to attack from the east, supported by flame-throwers and demolition teams. At the same time Maj Schoettel, who had finally rejoined his battalion,

Ebb Tide (Kerr Eby)
Eby made a tour of Betio Island when the fighting was almost over and came upon this scene on one of the invasion beaches. 'I was moved to tears,' he told *Time-Life* correspondent Robert Sherrod later.

was to swing 3-2 around the area west of the airfield to join up with Hays and completely encircle the enemy. The bulk of the close-in fire support was to come from half-tracks as most of the available tanks were engaged in the eastern end of Betio. The main strength of the defenses in the Pocket were facing the sea and Hays sent two half-tracks and a platoon of infantry out on the reef in an outflanking movement. The fire from these 75mm artillery pieces, pounding the complex from close range, and the determined assaults by the infantry with flame-throwers and demolition charges, finally wore the defenders down. A seemingly impregnable massive concrete pillbox facing the beach finally succumbed and this seemed to herald the end of effective resistance at around 1000hrs. Forward elements of Shoettel's and Hay's units joined up near the northern revetments of the airfield and swung north to finish off the remnants of the defenders. A small number surrendered, more committed suicide among the smoking debris and at 1300hrs Shoup was able to notify Julian Smith that the Pocket had finally fallen.

Messages confirming the collapse of enemy opposition on Betio were flashed to Harry Hill, Raymond Spruance aboard the *Indianapolis*, and

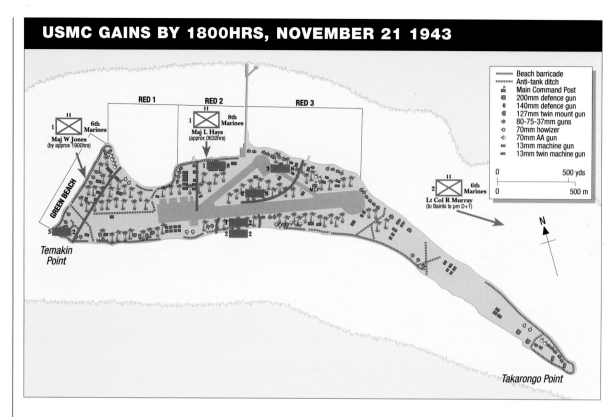

to Holland Smith and Kelly Turner off Makin. Of course this did not mean that all of the Japanese garrison were dead or captured; mopping-up operations continued for days as the Marines checked all of the burned and shattered pillboxes and bunkers.

At noon on November 24, Julian Smith and Holland Smith, who had arrived from Makin, witnessed a simple flag-raising ceremony as the Stars and Stripes and the Union Jack, to signify that Tarawa was a British possession, were raised on two battered palm trees.

Admiral Nimitz was to visit Betio later, and as he was conducted around the shattered moonscape and witnessed the carnage he could be in little doubt about what lay ahead in the 'island hopping' campaign across the Pacific.

All that remained was to mop up the remainder of Tarawa Atoll. It was known that a considerable number of enemy troops had swum or waded across the sand spit at the eastern end of the island and disappeared into the dozens of tiny islands that were strung out to the east and north.

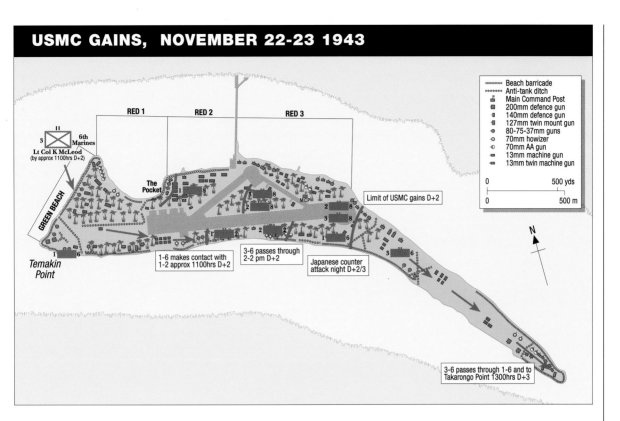

USMC GAINS, NOVEMBER 22-23 1943

Legend:
- ×××××××× Beach barricade
- •••••••• Anti-tank ditch
- Main Command Post
- 200mm defence gun
- 140mm defence gun
- 127mm twin mount gun
- 80-75-37mm guns
- 70mm howizer
- 70mm AA gun
- 13mm machine gun
- 13mm twin machine gun

0 — 500 yds
0 — 500 m

N

RED 1   RED 2   RED 3

3 — 6th Marines
Lt Col K McLeod
(by approx 1100hrs D+2)

GREEN BEACH

The Pocket

MCP

Temakin Point

Limit of USMC gains D+2

1-6 makes contact with 1-2 approx 1100hrs D+2

3-6 passes through 2-2 pm D+2

Japanese counter attack night D+2/3

3-6 passes through 1-6 and to Takarongo Point 1300hrs D+3

LEFT **Prisoners were rare on Betio, one exception was this officer, stripped to his loin cloth. Bob Libby, who described his hellish wade ashore on D-day, was standing a few yards away when this picture was taken. (National Archives)**

Although Col Raymond Murray's 2nd Btn 6th Marines had the job of tracking down these units, some preliminary reconnaissance work had already been carried out.

On November 21 elements of D (Scout) Company of the Light Tank Battalion, under Cpt John Nelson, had landed on the islands of Eita and Buota at the southeastern end of the Atoll where a radio station was located. Other elements landed north of the village of Tabiteuea on the eastern side.

Colonel Murray's battalion embarked in landing craft from Betio at 0500hrs on November 24 and headed for Buota to start their trek up the eastern side of the atoll to Na'a, the last tiny island in the north. Herbert Deighton, a Pfc with the intelligence section of Murray's 6th Marines, was one of the men who climbed into a landing craft at the end of Betio pier. He recalls that the troops were unwilling to depart from the beach as the tide was out and they did not want to wade among the dozens of floating putrefying corpses: 'We went across the lagoon to Buota and started to march from island to island; we did not make contact with the Japs but the villagers told us that they were just ahead of us.

'We were always thirsty and short of water, but were ordered not to drink from the wells we found in the native villages in case they had been poisoned. At low tide you could walk from island to island, but between tides the depth of water varied and in some places it was impossible to cross. We chased the Japs all the way up the Atoll until we were on the last but one island: Buariki.'

Murray sent out a patrol from E Company, while the remainder dug in for the night. The patrol clashed briefly with the enemy, killing three of them before losing contact. As soon as it was daylight, the rest of the

battalion moved forward and a fierce engagement followed in which 175 Japanese were killed. Marine casualties were not light: 32 dead and 59 wounded

On the morning of November 27 the navy and carrier-based aircraft pounded Na'a for around 20 minutes and Murray sent over a patrol. All that they found were torn up buildings. Their mission complete, the battalion embarked for Eita in the south for rest and reorganization. The battle for Tarawa was finally over.

The invasion of Makin and Apamama, the two other atolls included in Operation Galvanic, needs to be examined if the overall picture of the battle is to be understood. Task Group 50-2 – the fleet carrier *Enterprise* and the light carriers *Belleau Wood, Liscomb Bay* and *Monterey*, together with the battleships *Pennsylvania, North Carolina* and *Indiana* plus six destroyers – were the main components of the Makin force. Also standing by was Task Group 50-1: the fleet carriers *Lexington* and *Yorktown*, the light carrier *Cowpens*, three battleships and six destroyers under Adm C. A. Pownell, to counter any attempted intervention by Japanese naval forces from Truk.

The invasion force for Makin was provided by the US Army and comprised two battalions from the 27th Division's 165th Infantry under MajGen Ralph Smith. They were to invade the six-mile-long island from the ocean side and later in the day a third battalion would land on the lagoon side in support.

Men of 1st Btn 165th Infantry Regiment prepare to enter the jungle from Red Beach on Makin. (National Archives)

Major General Holland Smith had voiced his scepticism about the involvement of the army to Raymond Spruance, but he was overruled. The fact that 6,500 army personnel would be attacking a Japanese garrison of around 800 suggested to the V Corps commander that the operation should take no more than one day. In stark contrast to Betio, the army troops came ashore on Makin to virtually no opposition. The enemy had decided to dig in two miles (3.2km) inland and let the Americans come to them. At 1040hrs the 3rd Battalion came ashore in the lagoon, again to negligible opposition, and the three units joined forces and advanced to the perimeter of the Japanese defences. There the attack ran out of steam.

With no combat experience, the 165th Infantry were suffering the effects of a prolonged spell of garrison duty on Hawaii. Holland Smith, short tempered at the best of times, came storming ashore to see what was going on and was amazed to see tanks standing idle and troops lounging and awaiting orders.

When he arrived at Ralph Smith's HQ he was told that there was heavy fighting in progress in the north of the island. Commandeering a jeep, he drove to the scene of the 'battle' and found it, in his words: 'As quiet as Wall Street on a Sunday.' Makin was not to be secured for another three days.

This incident was the catalyst for a serious breakdown in relations between the Marines and the army that continued until well after the war. During the battle for Saipan in June 1944, Holland Smith had Ralph Smith relieved for 'lack of aggressiveness' when his men failed to keep

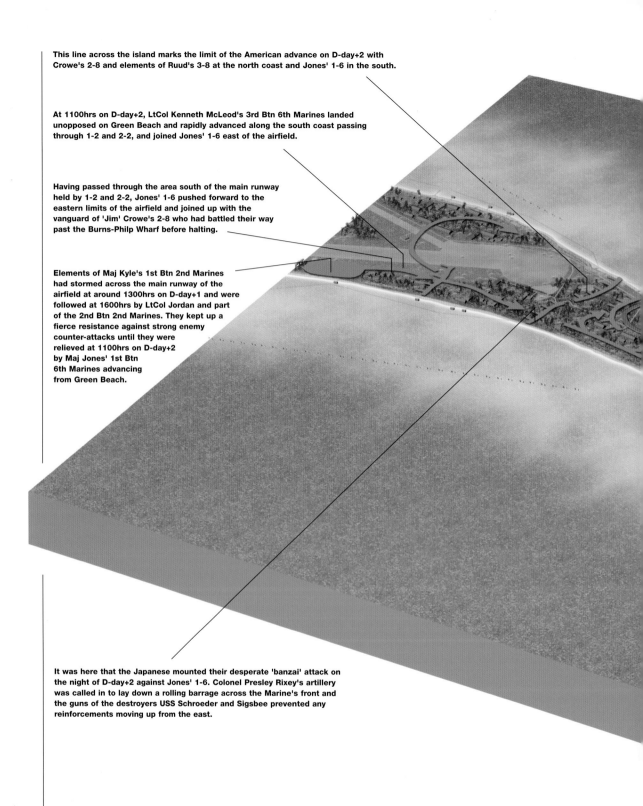

This line across the island marks the limit of the American advance on D-day+2 with Crowe's 2-8 and elements of Ruud's 3-8 at the north coast and Jones' 1-6 in the south.

At 1100hrs on D-day+2, LtCol Kenneth McLeod's 3rd Btn 6th Marines landed unopposed on Green Beach and rapidly advanced along the south coast passing through 1-2 and 2-2, and joined Jones' 1-6 east of the airfield.

Having passed through the area south of the main runway held by 1-2 and 2-2, Jones' 1-6 pushed forward to the eastern limits of the airfield and joined up with the vanguard of 'Jim' Crowe's 2-8 who had battled their way past the Burns-Philp Wharf before halting.

Elements of Maj Kyle's 1st Btn 2nd Marines had stormed across the main runway of the airfield at around 1300hrs on D-day+1 and were followed at 1600hrs by LtCol Jordan and part of the 2nd Btn 2nd Marines. They kept up a fierce resistance against strong enemy counter-attacks until they were relieved at 1100hrs on D-day+2 by Maj Jones' 1st Btn 6th Marines advancing from Green Beach.

It was here that the Japanese mounted their desperate 'banzai' attack on the night of D-day+2 against Jones' 1-6. Colonel Presley Rixey's artillery was called in to lay down a rolling barrage across the Marine's front and the guns of the destroyers USS Schroeder and Sigsbee prevented any reinforcements moving up from the east.

BETIO ISLAND, TARAWA ATOLL
NOVEMBER 23, D-DAY+3

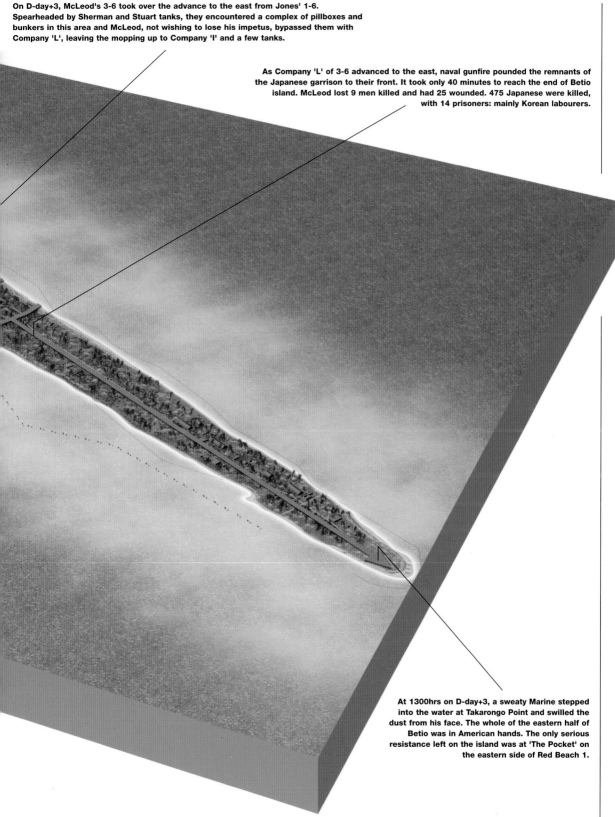

On D-day+3, McLeod's 3-6 took over the advance to the east from Jones' 1-6. Spearheaded by Sherman and Stuart tanks, they encountered a complex of pillboxes and bunkers in this area and McLeod, not wishing to lose his impetus, bypassed them with Company 'L', leaving the mopping up to Company 'I' and a few tanks.

As Company 'L' of 3-6 advanced to the east, naval gunfire pounded the remnants of the Japanese garrison to their front. It took only 40 minutes to reach the end of Betio island. McLeod lost 9 men killed and had 25 wounded. 475 Japanese were killed, with 14 prisoners: mainly Korean labourers.

At 1300hrs on D-day+3, a sweaty Marine stepped into the water at Takarongo Point and swilled the dust from his face. The whole of the eastern half of Betio was in American hands. The only serious resistance left on the island was at 'The Pocket' on the eastern side of Red Beach 1.

pace with the Marines on their flanks. The repercussions were felt all the way to the Pentagon and Holland Smith's career suffered as a result. At Iwo Jima he commanded Task Force 56 (Expeditionary Troops) in name only; the real leader in the field was Gen Harry Schmidt. Smith was also conspicuous by his absence at Okinawa, but the ultimate rebuff came at the end of the war when Adm Nimitz countermanded his invitation to the signing of the surrender documents aboard the USS *Missouri* in Tokyo Bay. Although he professed that he did not care at the time, he always considered this an insult to the Marine Corps.

It was the navy who were to suffer the heaviest casualties in the northern phase of the operation, with the sinking of the light aircraft carrier USS *Liscomb Bay*. The Japanese submarine 1-175 had been operating in the area for some time, and on 24 November was shadowing the *Liscomb Bay* in the hope of getting a clear shot. At 0600hrs the carrier came to general quarters and turned northwest into the wind to launch aircraft for an early morning strike. The turn brought the carrier directly across the bows of the 1-175 and she fired off three powerful 'long lance' torpedoes.

At least one torpedo struck the bomb storage compartment and every bomb exploded simultaneously, blowing off the whole stern of the ship. The resulting fires then exploded the fuel storage tanks and the *Liscomb Bay* became a raging inferno and sank in less than 23 minutes. The battleship *New Mexico*, sailing over a mile astern of the carrier, was showered with a ghastly mixture of debris, plating, aircraft parts and human flesh. 644 men died in the disaster including the Captain, R/Adm Henry Mullinex (more than ten times the casualties sustained by the army in taking Makin). Ironically, if the army had captured Makin in the single day that Holland Smith had expected, the *Liscomb Bay* would have been well on her way back to Hawaii on November 24.

A sweep of the area by destroyers failed to locate the 1-175 and she made her escape, having caused the northern operation's most serious

casualties. Apamama, a tiny speck some 75 miles (120km) southeast of Tarawa, had a small Japanese garrison and the Marines sent a party of 78 men from the V Amphibious Corps Scout Company to probe the defenses. The Marines embarked in Hawaii aboard the submarine USS *Nautilus*, one of the two submarines which had taken Carlson's Raiders to Makin 15 months earlier. After a scare off the south coast of Betio when they were fired on by a US destroyer, they arrived at Apamama, once the home of writer Robert Louis Stevenson.

The Marines landed in rubber boats and advanced along the six tiny islands that make up the atoll, killing one of a three-man Japanese patrol on the way. Local natives informed them that the main garrison of about 25 men were on the next island, so the *Nautilus* laid on a bombardment with her deck gun to soften up the enemy.

The next morning, November 25, all was quiet on the island and a native informed the Marines that the entire enemy garrison was dead. In a bizarre incident that reads like something from a comic strip, it transpired that the Japanese commander had accidentally shot himself with his pistol while addressing his men. The distraught troops, unable to make any decisions without their officer, had dug their own graves and shot themselves; the Marines were left to fill them in.

Once secure, the 'brass' arrived on Betio to study the defenses. Here Adm Nimitz (center) is accompanied by Julian Smith (front), and Gen Richardson (in peaked hat), followed by an assortment of officers including Merritt Edson. (National Archives)

AFTERMATH

With the battle over the 2nd and 8th Marines shipped out for Hawaii almost immediately; the relatively less-mauled 6th Marines stayed on to garrison the islands until they were turned over to the US Navy on December 4. At CINCPAC headquarters on Hawaii the 'inquest' got under way at once – the next amphibious assault was planned for the Marshall Islands in early February 1944 and the lessons learned at Tarawa had to be discussed and implemented straight away. Adm Spruance was eager to have the opinions of the 2nd Division commanders and of Harry Hill's naval team. They were not backward in letting him know what they considered were the shortcomings of Operation Galvanic.

There was universal condemnation of the use of warships as communications centers: the first salvo of the *Maryland*'s 16 inch (406mm) guns had virtually wrecked ship-to-shore radio links, and the portable man-pack radios had lacked effective waterproofing. On the plus side, the amtrac came into its own at Tarawa; had there been more of them most of the terrible casualties of the first day could have been avoided. After 'Galvanic' no assault landing in the Pacific took place

After the battle Marines march off to the transports.

without wave upon wave of amtracs leading the way. Better armed and armored, and with more powerful engines, they were the spearhead of every 'island-hopping' assault right through to Okinawa in 1945.

There was also much criticism of the naval bombardment of Betio, massive and sustained as it was. The Marines still had to face dozens of undamaged pillboxes, bunkers, and emplacements that had withstood everything that the navy could throw at them. The assumption that saturating the island with heavy gunfire would automatically silence the Japanese defenses proved to be a myth.

Other grievances were aired: the use of rubber boats was derided; there were queries about the coordination of the air strikes; and everyone complained about the tainted water. But towering above all this was the question of tides. Almost 50 per cent of the Marine casualties were sustained by men wading ashore in waist-high water from the reefs surrounding Betio. More amtracs would have alleviated the situation, but the decision to ignore the warning of Maj Holland was inexcusable: in giving priority to a pre-arranged timetable over Holland's advice the planners made their most costly blunder of the battle. 'Handsome Harry' Hill recalled a meeting of October 12 with Holland Smith, Julian Smith, Kelly Turner, Spruance, and Nimitz in which all phases of the battle were thoroughly discussed: 'The question of tides was discussed in some detail but I can recall no concern on anyone's part regarding the chances of severe consequences from a dodging tide,' he said.

The Japanese had performed well in the battle until the death of Adm Shibasaki, after which their command structure began to crumble. Severe casualties were inflicted on the incoming Marines from superbly constructed and ideally sited defensive positions. Had the admiral lived passed the night of November 20 there can be little doubt that a massive counter-attack would have been mounted against the precarious Marine foothold on the northern shore.

The image of the Japanese fighting man as myopic, ignorant, buck-tooth midget – as had been depicted in a continuous stream of Hollywood war movies since 1941 – was violently shattered at Tarawa. It was the newsreel coverage of scenes showing dozens of Marine bodies floating in the lagoon that shocked the American public into finally realizing the dreadful reality of total war.

Four Medals of Honor were awarded for the action on Betio, three of them posthumously Other outstanding achievements were recognized, notably the capture of Green Beach on D+1 by Maj Ryan and his gathering of the survivors of the landings on Red Beach 1. In retrospect, the capture of Green Beach was the single factor that turned the tide of the battle irrevocably in the Marines' favor, and gained Ryan a much deserved Navy Cross.

Despite the many errors and omissions, the battle was won in 76 hours of some of the most savage fighting of the Pacific War and it uplifted the spirit of the America people after years of depression. One newspaper heading read: 'Last week some 2,000–3,000 United States Marines, many of them now dead or wounded, gave the nation a name to stand beside those of Concord Bridge, the Bon Homme Richard, the Alamo and Belleau Wood – that name is Tarawa.'

MEDAL OF HONOR WINNERS

The Medal of Honor (sometimes mistakenly called the Congressional Medal of Honor) is America's highest military decoration and was awarded to the following combatants at Tarawa.

Staff Sergeant William J. Bordelon

Bordelon, of the 1st Battalion 18th Marines (Engineers), was from San Antonio in Texas and died in the fighting on D-day.

His commanding officer's report states: 'S/Sgt Bordelon, and Sgt Beers, with the other squad attached to "F" Company, landed as planned on Red Beach 2 about 125 yards [114m] west of the pier. Their LVT had stopped 15 yards [13.65m] short of an enemy 1.56 inch [40mm] gun and a heavy caliber machine gun, suffering heavy casualties. Capt Norris, Bordelon, Beers, and Pte Ashworth reached the beach, after which Beers was wounded, Bordelon was hit four times, along with having a blasting cap detonate prematurely in his hand. He refused aid and succeeded in neutralizing four enemy positions. He was killed destroying the fourth.'

In 1995, the Bordelon family had his remains transferred from the National Memorial Cemetery of the Pacific, in Honolulu, to Fort Sam Houston National Cemetery, and were afforded the singular honor of having his flag-draped casket lie in state in the Alamo in San Antonio prior to his burial.

Lieutenant Alexander Bonnyman

Close to the Burns-Philp wharf a sand-covered concrete blockhouse, defended by up to 200 Japanese troops, held up the progress of the Marines. Infantrymen, led by Lt Bonnyman, the second in command of 2nd Platoon 18th Marines and a veteran of Guadalcanal, charged up the western side of the blockhouse with demolition charges and flame-throwers. They killed the crew of an enemy machine-gun post and exploded TNT charges at the two entrances. The Japanese immediately counter-attacked from the opposite side, but Bonnyman remained at point-blank range preventing them from reaching the summit until he was killed.

At the age of 30, and with a family, he could have avoided military service if he had wished but chose to join the Marines as a private, gaining rapid promotion in the field prior to Operation Galvanic.

1st Lieutenant William Deane Hawkins

Though born in Kansas, Hawkins spent most of his life in El Paso, Texas. Several attempts to join the Army and the Army Air Corps were unsuccessful because of severe scarring on his body caused by a childhood accident. He finally joined the USMC in 1941, and a series of rapid promotions culminated in a field commission at Guadalcanal. At

Staff Sergeant William J. Bordelon. Landing under withering fire on D-day he attacked three enemy pillboxes putting them out of action and was killed while assaulting the fourth. (USMC)

1st Lt Alexander Bonnyman Jr who died assaulting the huge sand-covered bunker at the rear of Red Beach 2. (USMC)

Close to the Burns-Philp Wharf, a sand-covered concrete bunker defended by up to 200 Japanese troops barred the Marines advance across the east of Betio. Here, infantrymen and engineers led by Lt Alexander Bonnyman of the 2nd Platoon 18th Marines charge up the western side of the bunker and with flame-throwers and small-arms fire neutralize an enemy machine-gun position, driving the enemy from the top. His gallantry is to earn him a posthumous Medal of Honor (see page 85)

1st Lt William Deane Hawkins who secured the pier on D-day, and later died attacking enemy machine-gun emplacements. (USMC)

Tarawa he commanded a 36-strong Scout Sniper Platoon whose first assignment was to land ahead of the first wave of amtracs on D-day and dislodge the enemy from the long pier between Red Beaches 1 and 2. This was achieved after vicious fighting and he went on to lead his platoon in a series of assaults against strongpoints near the airfield. It was during these attacks that he was wounded in the hand when a mortar landed among his men killing three of them.

Refusing medical treatment, he led an attack on a series of enemy positions until he was hit in the chest and shoulder by a burst of machine-gun fire and died later that day in a field hospital.

Colonel David M. Shoup

Born appropriately in the town of Battleground, Indiana, Shoup was the only Medal of Honor recipient to live to receive his award. As operations officer of the 2nd Division he planned a great deal of the operation and because of the indisposition of Col Marshall found himself implementing his own plans.

Although wounded in the leg coming ashore on D-day, he set up his command post near the shore and continued to organize and direct the battle until relieved by Col Edson. He stayed on with Edson throughout the entire battle assisting with the implementation of operations.

Some senior officers, including Edson, disagreed with the supreme award, given his actual role. In 1959 he became commandant of the USMC, retiring in 1963. He died in 1983 at the age of 78 and is buried in Arlington National Cemetery.

THE BATTLEFIELD TODAY

Some 1,250 miles (2,000km) from both Australia and Hawaii, a visit to Tarawa is a long and difficult trip even for the most enthusiastic battlefield buff. Now part of the Republic of Kiribati, the Gilbert Islands are usually reached by plane from Hawaii via Christmas Island, or from Australia via Nauru (Yaren).

When the Marines finally departed in November 1943 the island of Betio resembled some weird 'moonscape' of craters, palm-tree stumps, and littered beaches; thousands of bodies lay buried in one square mile of earth, and the returning natives had problems recognizing the place.

In 1993, when a group of 2nd Marine veterans paid a return visit it was they who were amazed. Now luxuriant in greenery, the island contains almost as many inhabitants as at the height of the battle, but with the trappings of modern civilization; hotels, bars, shops, and a cinema.

There are still some remaining relics of the Marines' days of horror and triumph. Adm Shibisaki's massive concrete bunker, that resisted the navy's 16 inch (406mm) shells, now adorns someone's back garden –

A rusting steel plate command post near Takarongo Point. Originally this two-story structure, constructed of two layers of plate with sand between, would have had a swiveling cupola on top. (Jim Moran)

Fifty years after the battle, when these pictures were taken, Betio was luxuriant in greenery. This view from the west looking towards Green Beach shows that the cove is now largely filled in and the new concrete pier is seen on the left. (Jim Moran)

plans to turn it into a museum some years ago came to nothing. The bunker where Lt Bonnyman won his Medal of Honor stands behind the island's Police Station, and at Temakin Point the 8 inch (203mm) Vickers guns, now almost 100 years old, still stand defiantly pointing out over the vast stretches of the Pacific.

The wooden pier has been reduced to a few rotting stumps, replaced by a shorter concrete structure to the side, and the cove that was Red Beach 1 is largely filled in. The moldering remains of amtracs, anti-boat guns, and steel-plated command posts can be found by the wanderer, and a tiny section of the airfield remains in the grounds of the Maritime School.

Ironically the Japanese influence on Betio remains. The cluster of buildings at the end of the pier is dominated by a Japanese-owned frozen fish plant. A photograph of the 2nd Division war memorial being moved to one side to accommodate the fish plant, was shown in a Los Angeles newspaper some years ago; it indicates the changing values of 50 years.

APPENDIX 1

COMMAND AND STAFF V AMPHIBIOUS CORPS AND 2ND MARINE DIVISION

V Amphibious Corps

Commanding General   MajGen Holland M. Smith

Chief of Staff   BrigGen G. B. Erskine

2nd Marine Division

Commanding General   MajGen Julian C. Smith

Asst Divisional Commander   BrigGen Leo D. Hermle

Chief of Staff   Col Merritt A. Edson

2nd Marine Regiment	6th Marine Regiment	8th Marine Regiment	10th Marine Regiment
Col David M. Shoup	Col Maurice G. Holmes	Col Elmer E. Hall	BrigGen T. E. Bourke
1st Battalion	**1st Battalion**	**1st Battalion**	**1st Battalion**
Maj Wood B. Kyle	Maj W. R. Jones	Maj Lawrence Hays	LtCol Presley M. Rixey
2nd Battalion	**2nd Battalion**	**2nd Battalion**	**2nd Battalion**
LtCol Herbert Amey	LtCol Raymond Murray	Maj Henry Crowe	LtCol George Shell
3rd Battalion	**3rd Battalion**	**3rd Battalion**	**3rd Battalion**
Maj John F. Shoettel	LtCol Kenneth McLeod	Maj Robert Ruud	LtCol Manly L. Curry
			4th Battalion
			LtCol Kenneth Jorgensen
			5th Battalion
			Maj Howard V. Hiett

2nd Amphibian Tractor Battalion

Maj Henry C. Drewes

2nd Tank Battalion

LtCol Alexander B. Swenceski

This odd-looking device, still standing amongst the debris, is almost certainly a range-finder at the rear of a concrete Japanese gun emplacement. The bundle of clothing and pouches bottom left is the body of a dead Japanese soldier.

APPENDIX 2

JAPANESE GARRISON AND DEFENDERS' GILBERT ISLAND GARRISON FORCE

HQ–Betio Island

Commander RAdm Shibasaki

3rd Special Base Force	
(formerly 6th Yokosuka Special Naval Landing Force)	1,122 men
7th Sasebo Special Naval Landing Force	1,497 men
111th Construction Unit	1,427 men
(Detachment) 4th Fleet Construction Dept	970 men

Japanese weapon emplacements reported on Betio

Type	USMC estimate	Actually found Nov. 43	Size
Coastal Defence	4	4	8 inch (203mm)
"	4	4	5.46 inch (140mm)
"	6	6	3.12 inch (80mm)
Anti-Aircraft	4	4	5 inch (127mm) (twin)
AA Dual Purpose	8	8	2.73 inch (70mm) (twin)
Anti-Aircraft	12	27	0.5 inch (13mm)
"	4	4	0.5 inch (13mm) (twin)
Beach Defence & Anti-boat	6	10	3 inch (75mm) Type 94
"	5	6	2.73 in (70mm) Type 92
"	6	9	1.44 in (37mm) Type 94
"	16	31	0.5 inch (13mm)
"	17	?	0.27 inch (7.7mm)
For Tanks	14	14	1.44 inch (37mm)

APPENDIX 3

CASUALTIES

The Casualty Division of the USMC issued the following list in 1947.

US Marine casualties

	Officers	Enlisted
Killed in action	47	790
Wounded–killed	2	32
Died of wounds	8	82
Missing–presumed dead	0	27
Wounded–missing dead	0	2
Wounded in action	110	2,186
Combat fatigue	1	14
	168	**3,133**

Japanese casualties

Garrison strength–Tarawa	4,836
Total killed on Tarawa	4,690
Prisoners–Japanese	17
Prisoners–Korean labourers	129
Garrison strength–Apamama	23
Total killed–Apamama	23

The Japanese on Tarawa and Apamama suffered 4,713 killed out of a total of 4,859 (97 per cent).

The Marines suffered 990 dead. This figure does not convey the dramatic losses that some units suffered during the battle. For example 2nd and 8th Marines sustained casualty rates of 35 per cent; the 2nd Amphibian Tractor Battalion suffered 49 per cent casualties, and 66 per cent of the flame-throwers were killed. About 50 per cent of the Marine dead were killed in the water attempting to reach the beaches, and of the 125 amtracs, 72 were destroyed before reaching the shore.

The US Navy lost 644 men with the sinking of the carrier *Liscomb Bay* and an explosion in one of the 16 inch (406mm) gun turrets aboard the battleship *Mississippi* killed 43.

There were additional losses among the smaller landing craft and supply craft.

FURTHER READING

Alexander, Joseph H., *Across the Reef: The Marine Assault of Tarawa*, Marine Corps History Center, Washington DC (1933)

ibid, *Storm Landings*, Naval Institute Press, Annapolis, Maryland (1997)

ibid, *Utmost Savagery: The Three Days of Tarawa*, Ivy Books (1997)

Buffetaut, Yves, *Les Marines debarquent a Tarawa*, Historie and Collections, Paris (1995)

Gregg, Charles, *Tarawa*, Stein & Day, New York (1984)

Hoyt, Edwin P., *Storm over the Gilberts*, Mason & Charter, New York (1978)

Hammel, Eric, *76 Hours. The Invasion of Tarawa*, Pacifica Press, California (1985)

ibid, *Bloody Tarawa*, Pacifica Press, California (1999)

Russ, Martin, *Line of Departure – Tarawa*, Doubleday, New York (1975)

Shaw, Henry. I., *'Tarawa – A Legend is Born'*, Purnell's History of World War II (1968)

Steinberg, Rafael, *Island Fighting*, Time/Life Books Inc. (1978)

Sherrod, Robert., *Tarawa The Story of a Battle*, The Admiral Nimitz Foundation, Fredericksburg, Texas (1973)

Stockman, James R., *The Battle for Tarawa*, (Official USMC History), reprinted by Battery Press, Nashville, Tennessee

Vat, Dan van der, *The Pacific Campaign*, Simon & Schuster, New York (1991)

Wright, Derrick, *A Hell of a Way to Die, Tarawa 1943*, Windrow & Greene, London (1997)

One of the 284 Japanese who were killed on Makin awaits burial. (National Archives)

INDEX

Figures in **bold** refer to illustrations

1-175 (Japanese submarine) 80

airfield **25**, 25, 40, 56, **84**
Amey, Lieutenant Colonel Herbert 36
Apamama 11, 81
Australia 10

Betio Island **3**, **7**, 10, 22, **24**, 89-90, **90**
    defences 16-17, 21, 24, 25, **92**(table)
    pre-invasion bombardment 23, 26-27, 28-29, 83
    terrain **65**, **72**
boats, Higgins 22, 22-23
Bonnyman, Lieutenant Alexander 65, **70-71**, 85, **85**
Bordelon, Sergeant William J. 85, **85**
Buota 75-76
Butler, Ralph 31-32

Casablanca Conference, the, 1943 10
casualties 65-66, **66**, **67**, 72, 76, **76**, **93**(table)
    Japanese 69, **80**, **94**
    United States forces 32, 33, 37, **42**, **45**, **54**, 56, 60, **73**, 80
chronology 12
Colorado, USS 56
communications 37, 41, 43, 47-48, 82
Coral Sea, Battle of, 7th May 1942 10
Crowe, Major Henry (Jim) **34-35**, 40, 41, 58
currents 27

Dashiell, USS 28, 40, 49
Deighton, Herbert 75
Dutch East Indies 8, 9

Edson, Colonel Merritt 60, 61, **81**
Eita 75

Feland, USS 60
Fletcher, Lieutenant John 53
'foreign legion', the 22

Gilbert Islands, the 10, 11, 18, 22
Great Britain 8, 9
Green Beach **16**, 58-60, **59**, 84
Guadalcanal 10, 18

Hall, Colonel Elmer E. 55
Halsey, Admiral William Frederick (1882-1959) 14
Hawkins, Lieutenant William Deane 30-31, 86, 88, **88**
Heimberger, Lieutenant Eddie A. 53-55
Hermle, Brigadier General Leo 47-48
Hill, Rear Admiral Harry 20, 27, 28, 29
Holland, Major Frank 22-23, 30, 83

Indianapolis, USS 29
Japan 7-9, 9, 9-10, 10, **11**(map)
Japanese forces 18, 60, 64, 65, 68
    at Apamama 81
    assessment of 84
    'banzai' charge 68-69
    defence collapses 73-74
    effectives 17
    final message 61

Imperial Japanes Navy 8, 9-10, 22
    landings 29, 48
        Red Beach 1 32, 43
        Red Beach 2 33
    at Makin Island 77
    mentality 24-25
    opens fire on USS *Maryland* 26
    order of battle **92**(table)
    orders 21
    Shibasaki's death, effect of 52, 84
    Special Navy Landing Force (SNLF) 20-21
    suicides 66, **68**, 73, 81
    tanks 19, **19**, 21
Jordan, Lieutenant Walter 36, 42, 58

King, Admiral Ernest Joseph (1878-1956) 10, 13
Kingman, Rear Admiral H. F. 20
Kondo, Vice Admiral Nobutake (1886-1953) 16
Kusaka, Vice Admiral 15-16
Kyle, Major Wood 42

landings 24, **28**, 29, **30**(map), 30-31, **34-35**, **36**, **37**, **38-39**, **40**, 41, **46**(map), **55**
    Red Beach 1 31-33, 47
    Red Beach 2 33, 36-37, 45, 47
    Red Beach 3 40-41, 43
League of Nations 8
Leslie, Second Lieutenant 31
Libby, Bob 33
Liscomb Bay, USS 80

MacArthur, General Douglas (1880-1964) 9, 10, 13
MacPherson, Lieutenant Commander 29, 30, 43
Makin Island 10, 11, 22, 76-77
Marshall, Colonel William 15
Marshall Islands 11, 18
Maryland, USS 26, 27, 56
McLeod, Lieutenant Colonel Kenneth 61, 72
Midway, Battle of, 4th June 1942 10
Montgomery, Rear Admiral Alfred Eugene (1891-1961) 20
Moore, Ed 32
Murakami, Lieutenant 16-17

Nautilus, USS 22, 81
New Guinea 9, 10, 18
New Mexico, USS 80
Niminoa 54-55, 55-56
Nimitz, Admiral Chester William (1885-1966) 10, 13, **13**, 22, 23, 74, 80, **81**

oil 8
Operation Galvanic 11, 82-83

Pacific War, the 9-10, 10-11
Pearl Harbour 9, 13
prisoners 25, **74**
Pursuit, USS 28

Red Beach 1 31-33, 43-44, 47, **49**, 52, **54**, 83
Red Beach 2 33, 36-37, 44-45, 47, **48**, 52, 53, 56
Red Beach 3 40-41, 43, 44, 58
reefs 23, 25, 29, 20
Requisite, USS 28

95